S0-AAA-119

Marriage of Fire

Your Marriage and the Jewish Jesus

By David & Avi Epstein

Contents

© 2019 by David & Avi Epstein

Original Cover Art and Graphic Design by Avi Yiska Epstein

Scripture quotations marked (NIV) are taken from, and unless otherwise indicated, all Scripture quotations are taken from THE HOLY BIBLE, NEW INTERNATIONAL VERSION®, NIV® Copyright © 1973, 1978, 1984, 2011 by Biblica, Inc.® Used by permission. All rights reserved worldwide.

Scripture quotations marked (NLT) are taken from the Holy Bible, New Living Translation, copyright © 1996, 2004, 2007 by Tyndale House Foundation. Used by permission of Tyndale House Publishers, Inc., Carol Stream, Illinois 60188. All rights reserved.

Scripture quotations marked (NOG) are taken from The Names of God Bible (without notes) © 2011 by Baker Publishing Group, taken from GOD'S WORD®, ©1995 God's Word to the Nations. Used by permission of Baker Publishing Group.

Scripture quotations marked (CSB) are taken from The Christian Standard Bible. Copyright © 2017 by Holman Bible Publishers. Used by permission. Christian Standard Bible®, and CSB® are federally registered trademarks of Holman Bible Publishers, all rights reserved.

Scripture quotations marked (HCSB) are taken from the Holman Christian Standard Bible®, Copyright © 1999, 2000, 2002, 2003, 2009 by Holman Bible Publishers. Used by permission. Holman Christian Standard Bible®, Holman CSB®, and HCSB® are federally registered trademarks of Holman Bible Publishers.

Scripture quotations marked (NJCV) are taken from The New Jewish Covenant Version translation © 2018 of the Seven Covenants of the God of Israel (NJCV) open source.

Scripture quotations marked (BBE) are taken from The Bible in Basic English 1949/1964 (BBE) Public Domain.

Scripture quotations marked (GW) are taken from GOD'S WORD®, © 1995 God's Word to the Nations. Used by permission of Baker Publishing Group.

Scripture quotations marked (BLB) are taken from The Holy Bible, Berean Literal Bible, BLB Copyright ©2016, 2018 by Bible Hub Used by Permission. All Rights Reserved Worldwide.

Scripture quotations marked (BSB) are taken from The Holy Bible, Berean Study Bible, BSB Copyright ©2016, 2018 by Bible Hub Used by Permission. All Rights Reserved Worldwide.

Scripture quotations marked (NASB) are taken from the NEW AMERICAN STANDARD BIBLE®, Copyright © 1960,1962,1963,1968,1971,1972,1973,1975,1977,1995 by The Lockman Foundation. Used by permission.

Scripture quotations marked (GNT) are from the Good News Translation in Today's English Version- Second Edition Copyright © 1992 by American Bible Society. Used by Permission.

Scripture quotations marked (ABPE) are taken from the ARAMAIC BIBLE IN PLAIN ENGLISH, 2010 Copyright©, Rev. David Bauscher, Lulu Enterprises Incorporated, 2010.

One Fire

Introduction

God Made Ish and Ishah in His Image.

"Ish" is the Hebrew word for Man.

"Ishah" is the Hebrew word for Woman.

Few Christians know that "Ish" is also the Hebrew word for Fire.

So "Ish" is Man made in the image of the God of Fire, the God of Israel.

"Ishah" is the Female Fire made in the image of the God of Fire, the God of Israel.

Our God is a God of fire. (2 Kings 1.12)

He appeared in the burning bush. (Exodus 3.2, Luke 20.37)

He appeared in the pillar of fire -

"At morning watch, the LORD looked down on the army of the Egyptians from the pillar of fire and cloud, and He threw their camp into confusion." (Exodus 14.24 BSB)

The Lord is our banner of fire. (Exodus 17.15) The Hebrew word for "banner" can mean "miracle", and also "signal" like the pillar of fire.

He is a consuming fire -

Hebrews 12.29, Deuteronomy 4.24, Isaiah 33.14, Exodus 24.17 , Psalm 18.8, 2 Samuel 22.9, Deuteronomy 9.3, Isaiah 30.30, Isaiah 29.6, Isaiah 30.27, Joel 2.5, Psalm 50.3, Lamentations 2.3, Judges 6.21, Numbers 26.10

He sits on "a throne ablaze with flames." (Daniel 7.9 NASB)

No one should be surprised that the Hebrew word for "Man" and "Woman" is "Ish" and "Ishah" - which also means "Fire". We are all made in the image of Him who is a Consuming Fire.

It's no surprise that Man and Woman in their perfect created state were Beings of Fire - made in the Image of God who created them.

Jesus said "from the beginning" - Mark 10.6 NIV - "But at the beginning of creation God made them Male and Female."

In the very beginning, the first marriage between Ahdahm (which literally means the "blood kin of God") and Chavah (the "mother of all living") - was a Marriage of Fire.

Two beings of Fire united as One Fire.

Marriage is very different now than what Adam and Eve experienced in the garden of Eden with God walking beside them in the shades of trees (Genesis 3.8) - a couple not only put together by God but created for each other, in a world where death did not exist, adultery was unheard of, you had the best food at your fingertips that you didn't have to work for, and you could sit in the garden feeding parrots sitting on your shoulder.

Now it's two fallen human beings trying to 'figure it out' in a fallen and sinful world.

Maybe that's why now in many churches you hear people talking about how to 'get the spark back'. Not fire, just a little spark.

But know this - when two believers who are put together by God the Father marry, things *can* be different and they *can* have a marriage that's more than enough.

It won't be like the Garden, but it is possible to have a redeemed marriage just like the Jewish couples in the Bible. They experienced the Fire of the Spirit, even though the beings of Fire now wore clothes, instead of the fiery presence they used to have.

That's what this Book is about. To have as much as you can have in marriage in today's end times.

We're all descended from those two original Beings of Fire, we can dimly recall it, which is why we long for a Marriage of Fire.

Chapter 1

One New Flesh

It Is Not Good for Man to Rule Alone

God created Man and Woman in His own image, in the image of God He created them. He created them Male and Female, as Beings of Fire.

God blessed them and said to them - "Be fruitful, and increase, extend your rule, fill the earth, and govern it. I give you dominion over the fish of the sea, and over the fowl of the air, and over every living thing that is upon the earth." (Genesis 1.28 NJCV)

We see that God made Man and Woman, as Living Fire, to have dominion and rule the earth.

He put Man and Woman in the seat of power and authority over the earth.

Just before God did this, He had made Woman -

The Man gave names to all livestock of the pastures, and to the birds of the heavens, and to every wild animal of the fields. But for

Adam there was not found a partner to embrace and be an ally to him. (Genesis 2.20 NJCV)

The Lord said: "It is not good that the Man should be alone. I will make him a companion to support him." (Genesis 2.18 NJCV)

Then the Lord caused a deep sleep to fall upon Ahdahm, and He took one of his ribs, and from the rib the Lord made Ishah Ahdahmah a Female Being of Fire, and brought her to the Man. The Man said: "This is now self of my self, and flesh of my flesh. She shall be called Ishah, because she was taken out of Ish." Therefore shall a Man leave his father and his mother, and become joined together with his wife, and they shall be One Flesh. And they were both naked, the Man and his Woman, and were not ashamed before one another. (Genesis 2.21-25 NJCV)

This Being called "One Flesh" - One Fire - was given rule and dominion over the whole earth, because God saw that -

It Is Not Good for Man to Rule Alone

Jesus said it was not so from the beginning - in reply to pharisees asking if divorce was ok for any reason.

This shows that "marriages" that God didn't put together have been a big problem for a long time.

In the beginning - they shall cleave and become One Flesh - that's what a marriage was, One Being of Fire, with Spirits of Fire.

But remember, that statement was about a marriage where God brought her to him.

So what happens today if they cleave, but God had nothing to do with it? It was people's free will only?

It's a "marriage", but not a "what God has joined together" aka "one flesh" marriage.

God the Father gave Adam and Eve in marriage.

So by analogy when parents consent, is that the same?

God is our true Father and He knows best how to marry His children properly so that it lasts and causes no grief.

Look at the penalties under the Law of Moses for violating the holiness of marriage -

Adultery is death penalty.
End of conversation.

Under the Law of Moses, the penalty for sleeping together without parents' permission was the price of a virgin, probably about $100,000 in today's money - and the guy had to marry a woman and could not ever divorce her, which of course isn't the best idea of marriage because no one wants to be married to a resentful spouse, but at least women were valued for their feminine qualities.

There are people who would say that women have no business being a ruler or a matriarch, but look at 1 Chronicles 7.24 NIV: "His daughter was Sheerah, who built both Lower and Upper Beth-horon, and Uzzen-sheerah." This woman was a founder of three cities in the ancient Middle East. She did this during the times when there was no feminism, no women's studies, and women were often taken as slaves and captives. Does God give noble women strength and anointing? Absolutely.

Spiritual Warfare Battle Plan:

1. Remind God that you are created in His image, that you are a child of the Most High God, the God of Fire.

2. Every day, pray to God that He will bring you into a redeemed marriage of Spirit Fire just like the righteous Jewish couples in the Bible.

3. Thank Him ahead of time that He will do this, in Yeshua's Name (in Jesus' Name).

4. Start believing that you and your spouse can rule over everything in your life.

5. Find bible verses that line up with what you are believing for.

6. Say those verses out loud every day, and say that they apply to your marriage.

7. Keep doing these things until they come to pass. Don't give up.

Throughout this book you will see Spiritual Warfare strategies and Battle Plans like the one above.

They are based on Speaking the Word of God and declaring your faith in what God has promised you.

This is because You are a Speaking Spirit.

When you speak the promises with your mouth - your words will activate hidden mysteries in the Spirit realm.

After a few days, you will notice that your mind starts thinking "maybe I can do this, maybe this will happen". That's hope. Faith is the assurance, the reality, the manifestation, of things that you hope for but can't see yet. (Hebrews 11:1 BSB)

Good, keep saying what you are believing for every day.

Never stop saying it.

Your words are slowly turning the rudder of your life around to go in the right direction.

Your words are lining things up so that the winds of the Spirit are in your sails and propel you to your destination.

You will start to see things happen.

Your circumstances will start to change.

This is because you have changed things in the supernatural realm with your words.

The same way God changed things on earth with His Words - "Let light be, and light is." (Genesis 1:3 YLT)

So your circumstances must bow because they are only in the natural realm.

The devil wants people to think the natural realm is "reality" - but it's not - it's all controlled by the Spirit realm of the supernatural.

If your present 'reality' is less than blessed - it's because there is something evil trying to hinder it.

You can change it with your words, speaking the Word of God and His promises to you. Nothing can withstand the Word of God.

Chapter 2

Adam and Eve's First Argument

So things started off pretty good. Actually, God said it was "very good". (Genesis 1.31 NIV)

Adam and Eve never argued until after they listened to the snake (dragon, ancient serpent).

Their first spat was a blame game - Adam blamed his wife as well as God for the mess, she blamed the devil (which was true).

First rule of marriage - whenever things get messed up - put the blame where it belongs - on the devil. Marriage is about unity and accountability to a Covenant.

Spiritual warfare is the ultimate source of all human problems but no one feels like fighting battles when they are already exhausted and drained of enough energy.

God is the source of all human blessings and good things.

Don't blame your spouse when either one of you gets deceived by the devil. Find out where the deception is, and defeat it by the Name of Jesus.

Here's an example -

Wife to her husband - "Every time you talk to a particular person, I feel upset - I forbid you to talk to them anymore!!"

The wife may be accurate in pinpointing a source of demonic "static" - but her delivery of the message may just make it worse.

Better idea, same for guys when talking to your wife, "Hun, I have noticed that every time you talk with so-and-so, we seem to have an argument, or you seem influenced in a bad way. Can we pray for God to show us if there is some hidden issue with that person?"

Husband and Wife always need to be united together against all foes. But the devil wants to turn them against each other.

It always needs to be "us" figuring out whether "them" is a hidden enemy trying to disrupt our marriage unity.

That doesn't mean the husband or the wife may not be unknowingly influenced by spirits trying to work through other people. That's part of being a believer and dealing with spiritual warfare.

We have to always pray that our spouse has wisdom and discernment. If they get off the path, we need to help them get back on track. Blaming them won't help - since the source of all marital strife has only one source - the devil. He often uses people as a host to execute his wickedness, that's why you have to be careful about who and what you are bringing in the midst of your marriage.

Spiritual Warfare strategy:

Start praying at least once a week that your spouse will be given wisdom and discernment by the Lord Yeshua (Jesus).

Why is Marriage Different Now than it was In the Beginning?

Does it ever seem sometimes that Men and Women are at war with each other? They can't understand 'how the other one thinks'?

There is a reason for that. Adam and Eve were not created that way. Here's what happened, and we still have to deal with it today -

Both the Man and the Woman were called Adam before the fall. The Hebrew word for 'Adam' is 'Ahdahm', pronounced 'ah-dom'. Here is a glimpse into the ancient Hebrew words which open up secrets about that happened -

We can see this more easily by reading the following scriptures from Genesis 1 and 2 and 3 (HCSB) with the Hebrew words inserted in parenthesis for clearness -

Genesis 1.26 And God said, 'Let Us make man (Ahdahm) in Our image, in Our likeness, and let them (plural Ahdahm) rule, they (plural Ahdahm) are made to have dominion, they will rule (radah), prevail against, reign over the earth, and take all that is in it.

Gen 1.27 So God created man (Ahdahm) in His own image.

He created him (Ahdahm) in the image of God.

He created them (plural Ahdahm) male (zaqar) and female (neqebah).

Gen 2.8 The LORD God planted a garden in Eden, in the east, and there He placed the man (Ahdahm) He had formed.

Gen 2.15 The LORD God took the man (Ahdahm) and placed him in the garden of Eden to work it and watch over it.

Gen 2.16 And the LORD God commanded the man (Ahdahm).

Gen 2.18 Then the LORD God said, "It is not good for the man (Ahdahm) to be alone. I will make a helper (to surround and embrace, ally, protector, restrainer, support, relief in times of hardship and distress) suitable for him (in front of, in his line of sight, that he sees)."

Gen 2.19 So the LORD God formed out of the ground every wild animal and every bird of the sky, and brought each to the man (Ahdahm) to see what he would call it. And whatever the man (Ahdahm) called a living creature, that was its name.

Gen 2.20 The man (Ahdahm) gave names to all the livestock, to the birds of the sky, and to every wild animal; but for the man (Ahdahm) no helper (to surround and embrace, ally, protector, restrainer, support, relief in times of hardship and distress) was found as his complement (in front of, in his line of sight).

Gen 2.21 So the LORD God caused a deep sleep to come over the man (Ahdahm) and he slept. God took one of his ribs and closed the flesh at that place.

Gen 2.22 Then the LORD God made the rib (a primitive word meaning "to curve") He had taken from the man (Ahdahm) into a woman (Ishah, Female Fire) and brought her to the man (Ahdahm).

Gen 2.23 And the man (Ahdahm) said:

This one, at last, is bone of my bone and flesh of my flesh;
this one will be called "woman (Ishah, Female Fire)"
for she was taken from man (Ish, Male Fire).

Gen 2.24 This is why a man (Ish, Male Fire) leaves his father and mother and bonds with his wife (Ishah, Female Fire), and they become one flesh (basar echad).

Gen 2.25 Both the man (Ahdahm) and his wife (Ishah, Female Fire) were naked, yet felt no shame.

We we can see from the above that both the Man and the Woman were called Adam (Ahdahm, ah-dom). As One they were the Male Fire (Ish) and the Female Fire (Ishah) of Ahdahm the plural Being made in the Image of God.

Then this changed right after the fall -

And God said to Ahdahm,

Gen 3.19 You will eat bread by the sweat of your brow.

Gen 3.20 Then Ahdahm gave his wife (Ishah, Female Fire) the name of 'Chavah' because she was the mother of all the living.

Gen 3.21 The LORD God made clothing out of skins for Ahdahm and for his wife (Ishah, Female Fire), and He clothed them.

Adam gave his wife a new separate name 'Chavah' (Eve) because they were now separated from the Oneness they had before.

Remember in Gen 2.23, Ahdahm said: "This one will be called "woman (Ishah)", the Female Fire. That's what Eve was called before the fall, she was called the female part of Ahdahm (Adam). They were both 'Ahdahm' - he was "Ahdahm Ish", the Male Fire, and she was "Ahdahm Ishah", the Female Fire. So they were called together the same thing: "Ahdahm". They were not named separately. That's why it's still the custom for the Woman to take the Man's name in marriage - it's an expression of their intent to be redeemed from the curse and be like they were in the Garden, when they had a Marriage of Fire.

It wasn't until after the fall that Adam named his wife Chavah (kavah), which means -

The Mother of every life

Life giver

The Mother of all living

That's because there was a separation that happened from the perfect Oneness, when they both were Ahdahm together as One.

In Gen 1.27, the Hebrew word for "male" is -

zaqar זָכָר

That word can refer to both men and animals. It means the 'male of a species'.

It is associated with an ancient Arabic word zakar which can mean remember or call to mind something present or future and is found in verses related to -

kindness

granting requests

protecting

delivering

Such as Psalms 8.4, "What is man (Hebrew enosh, meaning friends, life, man) that You remember (zakar) him, the son of man (Ahdahm) that You visit him.

Now here's a major clue to a secret - the Hebrew word "adom", from which the name "Adam" comes - means 'red'.

This word also appears in such verses as -

Isaiah 1.18 Though your sins be red (adom) like crimson.

Genesis 25.30 Esau asked Jacob to feed him some of his red (adom) stew; the birthright was in the blood and was sold from Esau to Jacob.

2 Kings 3.22 The water was red as blood.

Genesis 9.6 Whoever sheds the blood of man, by man shall his blood be shed, for God made man (Adom) in his own image.

The Hebrew for 'the blood of man' is -

דַּם הָאָדָם

- pronounced "Dom haAdom", means literally 'the blood of the red Being made in the image of God'.

Thus Adam was literally 'the blood made in the image of God'.

Which is why the Messiah Yeshua (Jesus) came in flesh and blood, as the Sacrifice which took away the sin (which was red as crimson) of Adom (the red blood which was the life of the flesh made in the image of God).

Leviticus 17.11 YLT "For the life of the flesh is in the blood, and I have given it to you on the altar, to make atonement for your souls, for it is the blood which makes atonement for the soul."

Because 'the life is in the blood' - "Adam" means "life made in the image of God". So Messiah Yeshua (Jesus) came and gave His Life as a ransom for many to go free. (Matthew 20.28)

Isaiah 63.2 NIV "Why is your garment red like the one who treads out the wine press?"

Revelation 19.13 NJCV "His robe is dipped in blood, and His Name is called The Word of God. The Armies of Heaven follow him on white horses, they wear pure white linen.

Covenants between God and man are made by blood. In one sense the original creation of Man and Woman, Adahm and Chavah, was a covenant in holy blood.

That Covenant was for two Beings of Fire, Ish and Ishah, both of whom were One as Ahdahm, to live forever, even though they were flesh.

When they broke the Covenant, there had to be a sacrifice to restore our fellowship with God, our ability to walk with Him in the Garden in the cool of the day. And to restore our eternal life.

'Female' in Hebrew is the word -

נְקֵבָה

- neqebah (nek-ay-baw') which can refer to both women and animals, it means the 'female of a species'.

It's related to an ancient Arabic word naqab which can mean -

depth

spring of water

wisdom

leader

Since Chavah (the mother of all living) was taken out of Ahdahm (life made in the image of God), and since she too was made in the image of God, she was, like Ahdahm, 'blood made in the image of God'.

Now, Men and Women are almost like two separate species, no longer One as Ahdahm.

But because the Messiah came and redeemed us, Man and Woman can now be One in Yeshua.

That's our only path back to the Oneness that was lost.

That's the only Way we can have a Marriage of Fire put together by God Himself, the same Way He put Adam and Eve together.

Chapter 3

One New Marriage

Covenant of Oneness

This is the foundation on which you can build a solid relationship which can bring both of you great and lasting blessings in God -

You need to make a Covenant of Oneness with your mate.

You are One Person, One Flesh, One Being that was created to rule over the earth and everything in it. Find the places and things that God wants you to rule - and rule them for the Lord.

We have to be in unity with the Spirit of God inside of us. A house divided cannot continue to stand, and that's why many married couples are more roommates than rulers.

There's a prophet in the Bible who taught God's people about the concepts of material vs spiritual house. The Israelites were too busy eating, drinking, partying (sounds familiar to today's modern culture?), and putting all the work into their material homes while neglecting the call of the Lord to build a spiritual house, God's Temple.

"This is what the Lord Almighty says: "These people say, 'The time has not yet come to rebuild the Lord's house.' Then the word of the Lord came through the prophet Haggai: "Is it a time for you yourselves to be living in your paneled houses, while this house remains a ruin?" (Haggai 1.2-4 NIV)

Should we be deceiving ourselves while we are putting all the effort into remodeling our homes and spending our paycheck on spoiling ourselves and our spouses, while our spirits yearn to have a purpose in marriage?

Moving in a house and living together is where most marriages today begin and end. But God is calling us to deeper things -

"Go up into the mountains and bring down timber and build my house, so that I may take pleasure in it and be honored," says the Lord. "You expected much, but see, it turned out to be little. What you brought home, I blew away. Why?" declares the Lord Almighty. "Because of my house, which remains a ruin, while each of you is busy with your own house." (Haggai 1.8-9 NIV)

You have expected much from your marriage, but you gained little. And that little you had, God blew away. Why? Because you were too busy investing into a house which wasn't of God and where God's Spirit didn't dwell.

But once you begin to build the house which the Lord called you to build and set it up, you will take pleasure in it and be honored. Your marriage will be a beacon of light to others around you.

Spiritual Warfare strategy:

Ask the Lord to show you how to build the house of your marriage and ask God to dwell with you.

Chapter 4

How the devil fights against Marriages

Thoughts that destroy Oneness

God's plan for a successful marriage is the unity of heart, soul, mind, and spirit. The story of the tower of Babel speaks about people getting in unity in general but these verses can be translated to the marriage as well.

"The Lord came down to see the city and the tower the people were building. The Lord said, "If as one people speaking the same language they have begun to do this, then nothing they plan to do will be impossible for them." (Genesis 11.5-6 NIV)

Do you speak the same language as your spouse? Not just in the natural realm, of course you're going to marry someone whose language you speak and they speak yours. But on the deeper level, if as one couple you would speak the same language as your spouse, then nothing you as One plan to do will be impossible to accomplish.

What does it mean to speak the same language as your spouse?

Here are some of the clues:

Do you understand each other's meaning?

Do you walk in agreement with your spiritual beliefs and goals in life?

Are you both on Fire for God?

Are you both called to a ministry?

Can you relate to each other in emotional and intellectual ways?

Can you be honest with your spouse and communicate and work things out when there's strife?

Can you count on your spouse to be there with you as you both fight spiritual warfare in your lives?

Speaking the same language as one is very powerful and that's why we need to pay attention to our thoughts. Thoughts become words and words become actions and actions that you take determine how your daily life is going to be.

The Bible says a lot about the power of words (speaking things):

"The tongue has the power of life and death, and those who love it will eat its fruit." (Proverbs 18.21 NIV)

"The words of the reckless pierce like swords, but the tongue of the wise brings healing." (Proverbs 12.18 NIV)

"Gracious words are a honeycomb, sweet to the soul and healing to the bones." (Proverbs 16.24 NIV)

"May these words of my mouth and this meditation of my heart be pleasing in your sight, Lord, my Rock and my Redeemer." (Psalms 19.14 NIV)

We believe all these things literally, we believe what comes out of our mouths holds the power of life and death, we believe that wise people's words bring healing to us, we believe that pleasant words have the power to heal bones, to restore our bodies (if you don't believe us, just observe some people who constantly perpetuate their several diseases and sicknesses with constant negative and victimizing talk that just keeps them in bondage for decades).

So first, we have to watch our thoughts and where they come from. We think thoughts every single day and all the time. We even have thoughts at night, those are the dreams we dream (unless they are prophetic in some way inspired by the Holy Spirit).

Some thoughts are from us but some are from the deceiving spirits, (1 Timothy 4.1) demons (James 2.19) impure spirits (Mark 1.23) rulers, authorities, powers of darkness, spiritual forces of evil in high places (Ephesians 6.10-12).

Don't let those titles confuse you, there are different levels to evil spiritual forces so they are all not called one general name. Everyone knows about cherubim, seraphim, archangels, and angels but not many know about the hierarchy of evil forces.

How do we know specifically when the enemy is putting thoughts into our minds to destroy our marriages?

1 Corinthians 2.16 tells us we have the mind of Christ. If you are a born again believer, no matter what you did or didn't do in the past, you've been made a new person spiritually when you got saved and your mind has been renewed. (Romans 12.2)

Therefore, any thought that goes against your benefit in marriage that Christ would not want you to have is not a thought of your own. It's of an evil spirit.

"For I know the plans I have for you," declares the Lord, "plans to prosper you and not to harm you, plans to give you hope and a future." (Jeremiah 29.11 NIV)

God has a plan for your marriage, plans to prosper it, plans that won't harm you, plans to bring hope to your spirit, and a future which you can enjoy.

What are the devil's plans for your marriage?

To steal your happiness and peace in marriage, kill all the positive thoughts you have about your spouse, and destroy your marriage so you have wounds for a long time. (John 10.10)

We need to "take captive every thought to make it obedient to Christ." (2 Corinthians 10.5 NIV)

So we want you to start paying close attention to your thoughts. It takes some discipline at first but soon it gets a lot easier.

Why would you even allow the devil to teach you how and what to think? God isn't very impressed with the devil's thinking. If He was why would He say that satan will be thrown into the lake of burning sulfur to be tormented forever? (Revelation 20.10)

Let's say a thought comes drifting into your mind:

"Wow, what a great husband I have, he bought me beautiful flowers today, that truly blessed me!" or

"Thank God for my wife, she is making my life easier and better in so many ways!"

Those are clearly thoughts that no evil spirit would put into our minds because they compliment our spouses and make us feel happy and blessed.

But sometimes you might have some different thoughts: "I don't feel connected to my husband anymore, I wish I just left with another man long ago".

Is that a thought of the flesh or of an evil spirit? 1 Peter 5.8 tells us to be alert and of sober mind because the devil seeks whom he may devour.

He cannot devour you when you're at your strongest, because first he'd have to tie the strong man up. (Mark 3.27) Devils deal with us the most when we are at our weakest. The devil tempted Jesus when He was at his weakest, fasting for 40 days in the wilderness, hungry as a lion. (Matthew 4.1-11)

How come you feel the best thoughts about your spouse when everything is going good and you are being blessed day after day and you are strong in the Lord?

And how come when something frustrating or unfair has happened, or you had a fight or misunderstanding with your spouse, you think on so many negative and petty things about them?

It's not the flesh, it's a demonic attack against your mind. No evil spirit has a right to put anything in your mind because your mind is covered by the Blood of Jesus and the devil is illegally trying to get his way in and he may succeed unless you stop him.

Frankly, a lot of the things we think that we think of are actually "vain imaginations" and they are of the evil spirits. 2 Corinthians 10.5 tells us to cast such imaginations down. We will have to do it again and again, it's not a one day battle but it will improve your marriage for sure.

So if you have been irritated by your spouse or feel hurt or disrespected and thoughts are starting to come into your mind -

"I don't need her, I'll get me some better woman right away"

"My husband is such a loser"

"I am sick and tired of dealing with my wife's imperfections, she's not worth it anyway"

Then do this -

Spiritual Warfare strategy:

Whenever you feel any thought appear in your mind like the above -

Pause - think of Philippians 4.8 and say this out loud:

"These are not my thoughts! My thoughts are honest, just, pure, lovely, noble, and of good report. I think of only such things. Devil, I cast you out of my thoughts in Jesus Name and you are cast down in a pit of darkness where you can't see nor speak to anyone anymore. Cleanse my mind God and bless me with thoughts that align with the mind of Christ that has been given to me. In Jesus Name, Amen."

How the devil operates to sabotage your marriage, and how to stop him

We're going to look at the first example in the Bible where the devil was trying to destroy a good person and see how he operates.

Once you know what to look for, it will be easier for you to defeat the devil when your marriage is attacked.

First thing, the most effective attack is when you don't realize that the devil is trying to harm you. He for sure will try to make it look like he's "trying to help you" or "trying to warn you". This is what he did in the Garden of Eden -

Genesis 3.1-3 BSB tells what happened - "Now the serpent was more cunning than any beast of the field that the Lord God had made. And he said to the woman, "Did God really say, 'You must not eat of any tree in the garden?'"

The woman answered the serpent, "We may eat the fruit of the trees of the garden, but of the fruit of the tree in the middle of the garden, God has said, 'You must not eat of it or touch it, or you will die.'"

To see what was happening, we have to go back to Genesis 2.16-17 BSB - "And the Lord God commanded the man, "You may eat freely from every tree of the garden, but you must not eat from the tree of the knowledge of good and evil, for in the day that you eat of it, you will surely die."

God said this to Adam alone. It wasn't until Genesis 2.22 that Woman was created. So she didn't hear the command from God, she must have heard it from Adam her husband.

Maybe Adam added to what God had told him, or maybe Eve added "or touch it" when she was talking to the snake.

Either way, God didn't say they couldn't touch it, He just said that "you must not eat from the tree of the knowledge of good and evil". That's all He said.

Perhaps that is where the Orthodox Jews today get the idea of "putting a hedge around the Torah". This means "adding" a command by rabbis that was never in the Bible, in order to keep from going against an actual command.

An example is, the Bible says adultery is forbidden, so the rabbis say you can't even look at a married woman, the reasoning being that if you don't look, you can never commit adultery with her.

"You have heard that it was said, 'You shall not commit adultery.' But I tell you that anyone who looks at a woman lustfully has already committed adultery with her in his heart." (Matthew 5.27-28 NIV)

"I made a covenant with my eyes not to look with lust at a young woman." (Job 31.1 NLT)

It seems likely that Adam "put a hedge around the command", because Eve appears to have just been repeating to the serpent what she had heard from Adam (since she didn't hear it from God).

If so, that means that Adam was a righteous man who was going out of his way not to go against God's command. And he was taking extra care to protect his wife by warning her not to even go near that tree.

People understand that of course you don't want to put your hand in the middle of a campfire, so you know not to even get too close to it.

Eve had no idea the snake was trying to kill her. It is not written anywhere that either Adam or God had warned her about snakes. It doesn't say that God mentioned the snake anywhere either.

Unfortunately, because she was innocent, Eve couldn't imagine that anyone or anything would ever hurt anyone, or try to cause harm - she couldn't think like that or understand thinking like that - because she had only good thoughts.

That's why good people can be tricked by evil. They don't see it coming when it arrives in human form, because they themselves could never imagine being or thinking like that.

That's where evil gets the power that it has - surprise, trickery and lies. Most good people cannot imagine telling an out and out lie, they just aren't geared that way.

But that's exactly what the serpent did, it lied - "You will not surely die". (Genesis 3.4 BSB)

But before that, the serpent said to the Woman, "Did God really say, 'You must not eat of any tree in the garden?'"

That itself was a cunning misquote of what God had said. God only mentioned one tree they could not eat from. Eve answered correctly that "We may eat the fruit of the trees of the garden, but of the fruit of the tree in the middle of the garden, God has said, 'You must not eat of it or touch it, or you will die.'" And she added "or touch it" - which in her innocence she was declaring that she and Adam were being extra careful around that tree.

This whole conversation was designed by the devil to get Eve to focus on and think about the tree that God had warned Adam about.

One thing you can count on, whenever you "feel" something "pulling you" toward something you already know is bad - it's the devil every. single. time.

Maybe Eve in her innocent state could not have a moment of alarm, or even take a moment to think, "hmm, what's wrong with this picture"?

But we sure can. If a married man at his workplace is approached by another worker who tells him that a lady who works across the hall "is interested in him" - and if the married man is paying attention, he can see at a glance that the devil is speaking through the other worker to get him to focus on and think about a woman who wants to get with him.

If the married man says, "Sorry, I'm married", but then the other worker says, "Don't worry, just be nice and at least say hello to her, nothing will happen, it won't hurt anything" - the married man should run like the wind.

Because - the devil is trying to pull the married man toward the forbidden tree to kill him, wound his wife, and destroy his potential for God by making his life a living hell.

Sometimes people are "polite", they don't want to "hurt the poor girl's feelings", etc. But it's time to exit, quickly, firmly, and finally.

The next step is the married man meets the office girl, he doesn't understand that she has a demonic spirit of adultery, then she whispers in his ear, "Don't worry, no one will ever know". But God will.

That's one step away from a problem that can't ever be fixed. Marriages do survive cheating, sometimes... But the fact of it never goes away, "He who commits adultery with a woman lacks intelligence and is destroying his own soul. He is working to bring disgrace to himself and it overtakes him, and his shame will not be forgotten". (Proverbs 6.32-33 ABPE)

The same goes for murder. A demonic spirit of anger caused someone to lose their senses, for just a moment... right before they did something they can never undo.

Can the Blood of Jesus cover even these horrible things? Yes it can. God can forgive anything when someone truly repents from their heart.

But the memories of those things and the wounds they caused in other people are always there as a terrible reminder.

If you ask anyone who did something like that, they'll always tell you they would give anything to go back and *not do it*.

Some people deal with things like that and overcome them by warning others. You've probably seen former inmates speak at school assemblies and tell kids what they did, what it cost them, the pain it caused others - and they offer themselves as a warning to the kids to never do what they did. Those people who do things like that can overcome their past mistakes and have peace because they are living out their penance. God can redeem anything.

The best thing of course is never to 'eat of the tree' in the first place.

Here's how Eve could have seen it coming -

1. She could have refused to focus on the tree, or continue talking about it. When the snake asked "did God say?" - She could have said "Our time with God is our business, what He says to us is our

business. You are a snake and you should mind your own business. I don't like it that you want to dwell on things that God has warned us about, you should be talking and thinking about good things, pleasant things - why are you going on and on about something that will surely kill us? My mind is not a garbage dump for the devil! God said it! I believe it! and that settles it! So be gone!"

2. If she would have taken a second to think, "Adam and I already know there's something bad about this tree, because God warned us. We take extra care not to even touch it - so why is this creature trying to get me to have a conversation about it?" At the very least, Eve should've gone to her husband to tell him what's going on. Then they could have talked about it together. They could have discussed it with God later that afternoon when He came to visit them in the cool of the day. We would be living in a very different world today.

3. But she kept on standing there in the presence of evil. That's always a bad idea. Get away at once at the first sign of evil. That would have avoided what happened next.

"You will not surely die," the serpent told her. "For God knows that in the day you eat of it, your eyes will be opened and you will be like God, knowing good and evil." (Genesis 3.4-5 BSB)

The devil told Eve a lie, a big lie, an outrageous lie - which she failed to see, because she didn't leave right away at the first sign of evil.

So she was still standing there, a Woman of Fire, talking to a snake.

How many Christian women today, and men - are not aware of who they really are in the Lord - and have conversations with people who are not worth their time, not realizing they are on the other side of a conversation with the devil.

There are some conversations married people will do well to avoid.

For example, a person who wants to focus only on how bad their family members are, and how much they've suffered because of it, and then throw in a little bit about how good they themselves are. Anytime there's an accusation, you can bet it's the devil - because that's his name - "the accuser". In Hebrew the word for 'accuser' is -

שָׂטָן|

In English that word is literally pronounced "satan". It's Strong's Concordance entry 7854, if you want to look it up.

The same word appears in Arabic where it means "be remote, especially from the truth, and from the mercy of God".

And I heard a great voice in heaven, saying:

"Now the salvation, and the power,

and the kingdom of our God,

and the authority of His Messiah have come,

because the accuser of our brothers and sisters has been thrown down,

the one who was accusing them before our God day and night. (Revelation 12.10 BLB)

The devil is the one who is accusing you - even accusing you to yourself in your own thoughts. He stands behind people and speaks to them, "I'm worthless, I'm no good, I'll never succeed" - and believers don't realize the devil is writing the script. They think *it's their own thoughts*. But it's not, it's just the devil, lying as usual.

So anyone who is accusing other people, is speaking from the devil. It might even be a good person talking, but even good people can be deceived by the devil and speak for him. Like Eve...

Genesis 3.6 BSB - "When the woman saw that the tree was good for food and pleasing to the eyes, and that it was desirable for obtaining wisdom, she took the fruit and ate it. She also gave some to her husband, who was with her, and he ate it."

After she ate the fruit, and had died to God in that moment, what did she tell her husband? It was a lie of some kind, she was speaking for the devil. And he should have run away too, but he didn't. Did you know what Paul said about that -

"sin entered the world through one man". (Romans 5.12 BSB)

It wasn't over until the man also ate. That's because of two things -

1. Before they fell, Adam and Eve were Man together, one Being. Until they both ate, Man had not yet fallen.

2. However, after Eve ate she had fallen already. But Adam had not fallen. It wasn't until he made the same mistake as Eve, that he also fell - and that left earth without a Man or Woman who still had the Dominion that had been given to them by God.

So as Paul wrote, the man got to wear the shame and bear the blame for sin entering the world.

That's how the world came to be "under the sway of the evil one." 1 John 5:19 HCSB

Now that you see how the devil operates, here are some other everyday conversations where you can see him at work, trying to hinder and trip up believers -

1. People who don't want to talk about what you want to talk about. They want to talk about negative things, about how bad things are, they never quote the Word of God about how to overcome the world, etc. When you want to say something positive, they say, 'yeah, but'. Avoid them, get away from these people, give them no time, just section them out of your life.

2. People who just like to talk, endlessly, about themselves-. They're not your friends, you're just their audience. These

people are always bad news in the end. Trust us, we've met people like this. They'll say, "I want to help you", they'll give you compliments - as long as you let them keep talking, hour after hour, day after day. You will find that they can be more hateful than you could have imagined, sometimes with a big smile on their face. Remember that anyone who is your real friend wants to have a normal conversation and is interested in you, as well as wanting to share themselves with you.

3. People who say, "I have a word for you". They want to give you a 'prophecy' - only one thing - they have no evidence of the power of God in their life, and usually their life is a train-wreck. They love gossip and they want to tell you how they're a 'prophet' or a 'prophetess' - what true prophet in the Bible ever did those things? They are a 'prophet' all right - for the devil - whatever they speak will be false, and will be something that can cause doubt and confusion if you listen to them, such as - "God told me as long as you never go on Broad Street, you will always be blessed". What if God tells you to go witness on Broad Street? That means that so-called 'prophecy' was just to keep you from fulfilling God's Plan for you.

There's many more examples, but you get the picture - when you hear 'the accuser' talking, quit listening, and walk away - quickly. Before the snake bites.

How you can apply in your Marriage this knowledge of how the accuser works

Be ever alert for 'misunderstandings'.

That's often how an argument starts - one says something which is misunderstood by the other. The devil is right there shouting into their mind "see! he doesn't care! he doesn't respect you! I hate him!" Etc.

Have you been there before?

A few painful hours later, you both discover, oh my, that's not what he meant at all.

And you had a 'sore spot' from the past that he hit, without knowing it.

So you begin to learn to speak more clearly when talking of certain subjects.

And you learn the 'love map' of where your husband or wife has unseen wounds that still hurt.

And you apply the healing Bread of God to those wounds, and they get better.

And you realize that neither one of you can always be expected to know where every hidden wound is, every tender spot, every trigger point.

Because even the person with the wound may not realize it is there, until it is hit.

God can use these moments to heal you both. But you've got to adjust how you react when you first feel pain, and when you hear the voice of the devil telling you how much you are being wronged -

1. Try to hold it together for a moment.

2. Express what you are feeling - instead of speaking the accusations the devil is putting in your ear. This is not easy to do, but it can be done.

3. Say something like, "you really hurt me just then, do you know that?"

4. Hopefully your spouse will be shocked, and quietly listen as you tell him what is hurting you and how you feel.

5. Then hopefully he or she will say, "I'm sorry, I had no idea I hit a sore spot, and actually what I was trying to say was how wonderful I think you are." Once you hear your spouse's true intent, things change.

But what if your spouse actually said something hurtful, either carelessly or on purpose? Well none of us is perfect yet, and our tongues are set on fire by hell sometimes.

In that case, you're going to have to have as calm a conversation as you can, and the person who said the wrong thing is going to have to have to repent and try not to do that any more.

When two people really do care about each other, they can learn how to do this whenever they need to, and things will get much, much better.

Also, try to avoid the nuclear option. People who have been wounded as children, have the most difficulty with this. Someone once said, "never mess with someone who was an abused child."

When they feel they are being attacked, or when something reminds them of childhood trauma - they don't take the steps above, they don't pause, and they don't hesitate - they go straight to "Just divorce me, you don't care about me anyway." That's when they're being nice.

They can also go to a lot of cutting insults, and top it off with "I'm done. I want out. This is over. You blew it and can't get it back".

And so on. At moments like that, there is only one thing to do - and it's not keep the conversation going.

You have to get away from each other, then you have to go to God and use your faith to believe that He can bring peace where there is pain.

You have to then speak out loud to the devil and bind him, "In the Name of the Lord Jesus Christ I bind you devil in chains under darkness until the day of judgement, I forbid you to speak, I forbid you to try to influence me or my spouse in any way, I cast you out, you may go only to dry places and stay there."

Then ask the Lord to send mighty angels to carry away the devil(s) and take them where they can never come back.

You'll find that your Marriage will miraculously get better and you and your spouse will find healing from past wounds.

A big part of a Marriage of Fire is redemption. And healing. And miracles of deliverance.

When everything is going great, make sure you are taking thought to be kind to your husband or wife. Basic kindness is increasingly scarce in the 21st century.

Here are some simple ways to express your love and kindness in Marriage -

Your wife spends a lot of time and effort cooking so you can eat healthy meals - be sure you thank her for all that work - which some women hate doing - and let her know when she has made something that you love. Everyone appreciates it when someone notices something exceptional that they've done. Notice your wife and her accomplishments.

When your husband works his butt off every day doing 'boring stuff' that you're not that interested in, then takes you for a hunting expedition (otherwise known as "shopping"), be sure you let him know that you appreciate his hard work and thank him for letting you be female in a mall.

Many husbands think their wife is pretty, but never tell her because they don't want her to be "conceited". Not a good plan. Tell her how gorgeous you think she is, and don't just tell her once and think that's enough. It's really easy, just tell her when you're thinking about it, because then she can sense how you feel since you're feeling it right then.

Make sure you also tell her all the other wonderful qualities she has, not just looks. She needs to hear those things from you.

If your husband is clueless in some areas, tell him kindly. Most men will want to bless their wife. They just may not know that something bothers her. Or they may not know what would make her feel better if they did it. They can't read your mind, you have to spell it out for your man.

Women use indirect communication more than men do. So if you as husband want your wife to change something, remember that you're One Person. Don't say, "will you please stop doing" whatever. Remember that you and your wife are a team, and that the whatever is a third wheel - "Hun, can we think about starting to change whatever? It would really make me happy."

You get the idea. Don't take your husband or wife for granted. Let them know how much you appreciate and you value them.

That just slams the door in the devil's face. No devil can get through a Wall of Love. So Build That Wall.

Chapter 5

God Has a Purpose for Your Marriage

Spark vs Consuming Fire

We hear people in churches talking about 'getting the spark back'. They don't seem to know that the spark of infatuation and lust is usually gone with a year, two at the most. So if people got married because of the spark, that's going to be long gone soon enough, then what do they have left? If there is no purpose other than the spark, then divorce may be the next stop on the train.

Would you rather have a spark? Or a Consuming Fire?

God is a Consuming Fire. He can consume your marriage the way he did the burning bush that Moses saw.

If you're just a carnal Christian who wants to have sex like in the movies - and foolish enough to believe that's even real - then being consumed by God is probably not on your want list anyway.

However, if you are for real about pursuing God because of who He Is, then please know that your marriage can be filled with the Fire of God. That was His plan from the Beginning.

Marriage is supposed to have a purpose. You may not know exactly what it is yet, but if God put you and your spouse together, you know there is a purpose because there is a purpose to everything that God does.

Do you think Jacob knew anything about Judah his son-to-be when he had just married a woman - Leah - who was created for him though he didn't even want her to begin with? Judah was the forefather of Jesus, and even though Judah's mother Leah wasn't loved (Genesis 29.31) by her husband, the anointing that God put on her was still burning like a fire and she had six sons. (Genesis 30.20) It's quite possible that when her own sister Rachel died, she as the aunt had to now take care of her sister's two boys. That's how much God trusted Leah.

God has a purpose for every believer in Yeshua the Jewish Messiah. That means that God has a purpose for every marriage of believers in Yeshua the Jewish Messiah.

So our question is this - why does the church follow the worldly culture today when it comes to marriages? Why are churches knowingly or unknowingly trying to get believers to want what Samson and Delilah had instead of what Isaac and Rebecca had?

Why do christians feel okay with settling for "a spark" instead of a Marriage created in God's Image - a Consuming Fire? (Hebrews 12.29)

Fire purifies you from the inside out like it purifies gold and silver (Malachi 3.3). It cleanses you, it burns away any ties that shouldn't be there and any godless thought/thing in your life.

Sparks don't last long and in the cold of the winter when troubles come and marriage gets tough, that spark soon vanishes. When Isaiah 5.20 talks about calling evil good and good evil in the last days, it means that the time will come (and it's been here for quite some time) that people (yes, even believers) will lack the gift of discernment. Don't be easily led astray by a Samson and Delilah type of romance, it doesn't last but for a brief time and in the end brings sorrow with it.

"As iron sharpens iron, so one person sharpens another." (Proverbs 27.17 NIV) We don't know about you but we're not satisfied with a spark, we'd rather have a Blazing Fire type of Supernatural Marriage.

God showed Himself to the Israelites in/as the Pillar of Fire (Exodus 13.21) - not as a fading spark.

In fact, God was so radiant that Moses' face was completely changed:

"When Aaron and all the Israelites saw Moses, his face was radiant, and they were afraid to come near him. But Moses called to them, so Aaron and all the leaders of the community came back to him, and he spoke to them. Afterward all the Israelites came near him, and he gave them all the commands the Lord had given him on Mount Sinai. When Moses finished speaking to them, he put a veil over his face. But whenever he entered the Lord's presence to speak with him, he removed the veil until he came out. And when he came out and told the Israelites what he had been commanded, they saw that his face was radiant. Then Moses would put the veil back over his face until he went in to speak with the Lord." (Exodus 34.30-35 NIV)

If you allow God - who is the Wisest and Everlasting - to pick your spouse just like He did for Jacob and Isaac and Boaz and some others, He will transform your life and cover you with His Light and Brilliance.

Notice that Moses didn't even remove the veil among his people, he would only remove it while talking face to face with God.

When there is a huge lack of healthy teaching about beginning a marriage in today's church yet churches have a bad attitude towards a divorced person - they are completely out of God's will.

Some believers use the verse "what God has joined together, let no one separate" (Mark 10.9 NIV) as a sledgehammer towards anyone considering a divorce - but consider if they may be doing it wrongly.

Notice that it says "_what GOD has joined together_, let no one separate" - not what two persons chose to join together.

So in what context does God say: "I hate divorce". (Malachi 2.16 BSB) In the context of Him bringing two people supernaturally to each other for a higher purpose.

The full truth is, see if you can find a verse where God ever said anything about two people who made a mistake to be with each other not divorcing. He simply spoke about marriage that He Himself joined together. Again, read the scriptures for yourself, these are just our thoughts. Even if two people who made a mistake divorce, it's still painful and hurtful, and no one would ever think it's a good thing. But if two people who were never meant to be together are ripping each other apart, then from the standpoint of love and peace, divorce may actually be kinder than staying together. In the Beginning, God put them together - that was the best way then - and it's the best way now.

There are a few people who say that if two people marry, then God joins them together, in the sense that if anyone gets married, then God recognizes that. If that were the case, how would there be any difference then between a marriage that God Himself put together, and a 'marriage' that two people chose for the wrong reasons? Those are two different kinds of marriages, the true and the false. A few preachers have even said that whenever any two people just have sex, then that is a 'marriage'. Really? If it is, then it's a really bad copy of the real thing.

God hates divorce, that's for sure. But suppose if there was a marriage where two unbelievers got married because they liked having sex while they were doing drugs together. Later the spark went out, and they both cheated on each other and the husband was beating up the wife. Would God hate it if they split? Would He like it better for the woman to keep getting beat up? Think it through - God is Love, He doesn't want women to get beat up (or children either). What God would like is if the two of them got saved, repented, and began loving each other. But that's up to them because they have free will. In addition, if two unbelievers 'marry', neither of them has recognized God, so why should He recognize their 'marriage'? Just something to think about.

Sarah was the Mother of nations and the Mother of kings (Genesis 17.16). God named her Sarah, the Princess, a woman of high rank, a noblewoman.

Rebecca's son and grandsons and great-grandsons possessed the gates of their enemies (Genesis 24.60).

Leah had Judah who was her fourth son (Genesis 29.34-35) and Jesus the Jewish Messiah came through him.

These ladies' children were "children born not of natural descent, nor of human decision or a husband's will, but born of God." (John 1.13 NIV) Why did Abraham send away all of his children except Isaac? Because Isaac was the one born from God's will, God's Holy Spirit.

These are just a few examples of a higher purpose in a marriage. Good sex isn't a purpose, having whatever wife you "fall in love" with isn't a purpose, having a car or a house or a diamond ring isn't a purpose.

Does your marriage have a divine purpose?

Or did you marry someone you just 'fell in love' with and you regretted it later on? Did you let your heart lead you to the 'right' person because, if you did, remember this: "The human heart is the most deceitful of all things, and desperately wicked. Who really knows how bad it is?" (Jeremiah 17.9 NLT) That means that even your Pastor doesn't know your heart. Only God does.

Do you know of anyone who "let their heart lead them" to their spouse? How did that work out? We all know people like that, and so many, many times it ends in disaster.

How many people do you know who have been "unlucky in love" every time? Where have all the good men/women gone? They may have just been deceived by their own heart and flesh.

Only God knows the future.

Only God knows every detail about every person.

Only God can know the person you will be right for and who will be right for you - and together you will fulfill God's purpose for both of you.

Forget the worldly garbage of following your emotions and lust, let the Holy Spirit lead you to the person who He created to be your helpmate, give up your will completely if you truly desire to be in the center of God's will.

The more you give up your will in the area of marriage and the more you receive God's will, the happier and more blessed you both will be.

Surely not every decision we Christians make has been God ordained - or those decisions would lead to blessing.

Remember that deceitful and rotten friend you befriended as a Christian, who wasn't God ordained? That immature selfish spouse you married that you later divorced who wasn't God ordained? That business partner who cheated you, because you "felt" good about being in business with him? Were those relationships God ordained - or *you*-ordained? Here's what the bible says about that -

All a man's ways seem right to him, but the Lord evaluates his true motives. (Proverbs 21.2 HCSB)

There is a way that seems right to a man [in his desperately wicked heart], but its end is the way to death. (Proverbs 14.12 HCSB and Proverbs 16.25 HCSB)

God doesn't get pleasure if you to live with a wife who is always destroying your peace and your ability to work, and dragging you both down. Or a husband who is beating you or cheating on you. Let's be honest, if that's the situation, God never put that marriage together. So does He condemn anyone who divorces from an ungodly spouse? That's a question you'll have to answer for yourself. It's not about the spark anyways, it's about a purpose.

Spiritual Warfare Strategy:

Start praying every day that God will reveal to you the purpose of your marriage, and ask Him to bring His Will to pass for your marriage.

Ask Him for a Marriage of Fire - consumed by His Fire - not by the cares and things of the world and what 'other people think'.

Chapter 6

What if you already married #2 (or even #32)?

God loves you more than he hates divorce

Divorce has always been a sensitive subject in Jewish/Christian communities. In today's instant gratification society where we want things fixed immediately or thrown aside, we have to know that God isn't done with our marriages simply because things haven't been perfect yesterday or the day before. In today's culture of "why buy the cow when I can get the milk for free", it's important to teach women to raise their bar higher because a righteous man will climb the wall no matter how high it is for the woman God truly has for him.

Our reading of the bible is -

The One Flesh Marriage is a redeemed Marriage of Fire that God has put together for a higher shared purpose.

It's ok to get married young.

It's also fine to remain single if that is your wish, so you can devote yourself to the things of God and to whatever ministry the

Lord gives you to do. Sometimes single people get so busy in a ministry that they are surprised one day when God brings them together with the true mate that He has chosen for them.

Since it's better to get married than to lust all day - every unmarried believer who wants marriage should be praying before the Throne asking God to put him/her together with the right person. This will produce a supernatural marriage, the kind that Isaac and Rebecca had, and that Ruth and Boaz had. Ruth was called a virtuous woman. She didn't marry because of a 'spark' or because she was 'in love'. She married a good man, a man known in the gates of the city, who was wise enough to know that he had found a woman "far above rubies" that he could cherish her, take good care of her, and praise her for her virtue.

But what if you sense that you are held back because of the person you married?

If you have a marriage where you both got married because of 'the spark' - then later drifted apart, a marriage where one reads the bible, one doesn't, there is no shared purpose, there is constant insult and misery, and the two are not in agreement in most major areas -

Amos 3.3 (BSB) "Can two walk together without agreeing where to go?"

Such a couple is not in the right plan of marriage because they have not agreed on goals and certainly are not fulfilling God's purposes for them.

In any case, if there has to be a separation or divorce, it should be done in peace - not stalking, divorce rape, turning the children against the other parent, trying to steal assets, etc.

Where God has not put something together and it's robbing one or both parties of their potential in God, then the civil court which put it together can undo it, because the legal "piece of paper" of marriage can be ended by the same authority that gave it.

But a civil court cannot create two hearts into one, nor make "one flesh" of two people. Because a worldly court cannot create a One Flesh marriage, only God can do that.

Neither can a civil court make two out of what has been made one by God. A court cannot separate what God has made One.

The law of Heaven is "What God has joined together, let not man separate". (Matthew 19.6 BSB)

If God has joined two people together and they have a falling out, one or both of them must repent and get back on track because God's calling, purpose, and anointing is on their marriage.

But what if two people put themselves together instead of God doing it? Even so, if they're believers they can still agree to walk as one in God's purpose for them - and if they give up their own will and find out what God can do with the situation - He can still fix anything if both people truly seek Him and use only the Word of God for every answer they need.

But only if both parties want to work on it do you have a chance. That's because each party has free will. If they get into agreement then they can have a good marriage in God. If one of them is not in agreement to work it out, then how can two walk together if they are not in agreement?

And if one party is not willing to follow the Bible to work on it then have they left the marriage? Paul says if the unbeliever wants to leave, let them leave. The Aramaic for 'unbeliever' can mean one who 'does not believe, is not trustworthy, has changed a promise'.

Paul phrases the situation in an interesting way, "To the married I give this command (not I, but the Lord): A wife must not separate from her husband. But if she does, she must remain unmarried or else be reconciled to her husband. And a husband must not divorce his wife. *To the rest I say this...(I, not the Lord)...* 1 Corinthians 7.10-12 NIV   If any brother has a wife who is not a believer and she is willing to live with him, he should not divorce her. And if a woman has a husband who is not a believer and he is willing to live with her, she should not divorce him.

However, what Paul says there - as his own opinion *(I, not the Lord)* - differs from Ezra 10.11 (NIV), where the Israelites who had married unbelievers, were told by Ezra, "Now honor the Lord and do his will. Separate yourselves from your unbelieving wives."

Paul does not say whether any of the brothers had a wife who was not a believer, and who was worshiping baal or other pagan god, or otherwise hindering the believing husband from his walk with God. Maybe Paul's opinion implies that he's talking only about upstanding moral people who are not believers yet, and Paul as an evangelist is hoping they will get saved. One assumes that was the case, since Paul would not say anything that conflicted with other scripture.

Note that when Paul "gives a command", sometimes it is from the Lord (and he indicates that), and sometimes it is just his own opinion (as he said in the verse above).

Paul first gives God's command "To the married..." Then Paul gives his own opinion "To the rest..." Does this mean that only believers can actually be married? That "the rest" are not married in God's sight?

Does a "believer" mean someone who just says that he is one?

Or does it mean someone who, in spite of mistakes, is actively studying the bible and trying to do what Jesus says?

For example, what do you think about these two couples:

Couple 1 The pray together regularly, read the bible regularly, and in their hearts are sincerely trying to follow Jesus in the light that they have. But they constantly don't get along. Yet they really want to have a good marriage.

Couple 2 one spouse prays, reads the bible, and is trying to follow the Lord. The other spouse doesn't really care about those things. They both don't get along. The spouse who prays wants to have a good marriage, but the other spouse doesn't care, refuses to try, and instead actively criticizes the other and shuts them out.

So if both couples when they married promised to try to work on their marriage and stay married, but the spouse in Couple 2 decided to change that promise and reject the marriage, does that mean the other spouse can leave and remarry?

Or does it mean that any spouse can decide they don't want to actively seek God and work on their marriage? And if they do, and their rejected spouse is then forced to separate - is the rejected spouse then stuck with not remarrying? Or is this the situation where Paul says that the 'promise breaker' can depart and the other spouse is free to remarry?

It's interesting to wonder if one spouse can be bound by the other's free will decision to go against what the bible says. In other words, it is clear that husband and wife are to join together in unison and prefer one another. But if one free will decides not to do that, is the other one's option to remarry prevented by the one who won't do what the bible says? Or is it the case that if one spouse persists in refusing to do what the bible says to have a Covenant of Oneness with their spouse, then their spouse can separate and remarry?

There will be a lot of controversy over this chapter.

Our purpose here is not to tell anyone what to do, but just to help people think about this very difficult problem.

All we can say is "pray about it".

And think about it - why is there so much divorce today? Is it because God put all those marriages together? Or is it because people choose to put themselves together and it eventually falls apart?

Why is there so much cheating? Not because God put two people together.

Why are so many marriages miserable and not accomplishing the purposes of God? It can't be because God put all those people together.

It depends on what you believe a "marriage" is. Is marrying someone you choose and getting a judge to give you a "piece of paper" - a marriage? Some people say yes.

Or is that one step better than just shacking up?

Why are so many skipping "marriage" today and just shacking up instead? Is it because they intuitively know that what they have isn't a biblical marriage anyway? Because they know it's not likely to work? Because if someone "is not in the relationship", they want to be able to move on without ripping each other to pieces?

70% of all divorces between Christians today are filed by the wife. It's not possible that all the men in those marriages were horrible husbands and fathers. It just so happens that couples get saturated with one another and have enough of each other's presence.

Here's what Paul says 1 Corinthians 7.10-11 NIV:

"A wife should not depart from her husband. And if she does depart, let her remain without a husband or let her be reconciled to her husband and let not a man forsake his wife."

We are in no way recommending divorce. Use a lot of discernment before marrying someone and use it before divorcing someone. Talk to people who have the power of God operating in their lives. Not your "friends" who don't show any gifts of the Spirit. But people who are wise and discerning, and who operate in love, because you want to get this decision right.

Above all, get before the Lord, and wait until He shows you by Scripture, by signs, by words from other people, and other ways, what you should do.

If you're already divorced, please know that God loves you more than he hates divorce. You can start right now believing God for the person He has chosen for you. He can make things as good as they were bad. Leave the past behind and press forward to the purposes God has for you.

Spiritual Warfare Battle Plan:

If you're in a marriage of great distress, make plans to seek God every day until He shows you what to do.

Even if you have no faith and no hope, God says that by simply "wearing Him out" until you get the answer, He's fine with that.

Luke 18.6 (CSB) - Now Yeshua (Jesus) told them a parable on the need for them to pray always and not give up. "There was a judge in a certain town who didn't fear God or respect people. And a widow in that town kept coming to him, saying, 'Give me justice against my adversary.'

"For a while he was unwilling, but later he said to himself, 'Even though I don't fear God or respect people, yet because this widow keeps pestering me, I will give her justice, so that she doesn't wear me out by her persistent coming.' "

Then the Lord said, "Listen to what the unjust judge says. Will not God grant justice to his elect who cry out to him day and night? Will he delay helping them? I tell you that he will swiftly grant them justice."

Chapter 7

How to Marry the #1 Best Person for You

Let God Choose Your Spouse

How many times have you heard someone talking about a list of things they want in a mate - a list of 10 or 20 things, sometimes 30 things - but that's transactional, not relational.

It's just checking things off the list – it's the whole "test taking" culture/system in the US. You're supposed to know "the right answers", but nobody ever teaches you "the right questions" to ask in the first place.

Many believers marry a list - instead of a person. They marry their choice of things on a list - instead of God's choice for them. It's usually someone that had "7 out of 10" things on their list -

already admitting that even by their own "list", it is not a perfect "choice".

A year or two after the marriage, they finally meet the person they actually married, now that no one is putting their best foot forward. It may take that long to really even begin to get to know someone.

Is there any wonder how many believers get divorced? The wonder is that the divorce rate is *only* 50%. And that may be because there are so many "regular" people who could get along with most anyone that it just works out sometimes by the law of averages.

In the beginning it was this "They shall cleave (be united) and become one flesh". (Genesis 2.24 NIV)

But remember, that statement was about a marriage where God brought a woman (Eve) to a man (Adam).

It's interesting to realize that Adam never witnessed God taking his rib out to create Eve, because Adam was asleep (did he sleep each night also, before the fall?)

Adam simply believed what God had said that she was taken from his body.

Adam, in his perfect created state, believed God, by faith.

That's what God was looking for when he found Abraham. Faith is a divine attribute that God creates us to have, faith in the God of Fire for a blessed marriage.

So what happens today if they cleave, but God had nothing to do with it, it was simply their free will? It's a "carnal marriage", but not a "what God has joined together marriage".

You cannot rely on something so temporary as a "spark" to make a long lasting decision - if you want to marry one time and stay married for the rest of your life, then allow God's Spirit to be the "matchmaker" on your behalf, because God doesn't want third or fifth best for you, He wants only *the* best.

God the Father gave Eve to Adam in marriage.

So by analogy when parents consent, is that the same? It can be, but only if the parents are led by the Spirit of God and not of their own fleshly desires of wanting to have grandchildren or paying less bills for an unmarried son or daughter.

Adultery had a death penalty for violating the holiness of marriage, and it surely causes the death of trust between two spouses:

"Marriage should be honored by all, and the marriage bed kept pure, for God will judge the adulterer and all the sexually immoral". (Hebrews 13.4 NIV)

Did you know that craving the wrong thing can become your grave? "But while the meat was still between their teeth and before it could be consumed, the anger of the LORD burned against the people, and He struck them with a severe plague. Therefore the place was named Kibroth Hattaavah, because there they buried the people who had craved other food." (Numbers 11.33-34 NIV)

If you are craving something that's out of God's will, be careful. You don't want to end up like the Israelites who lusted after meat and despised manna which was "the bread of angels". (Psalm 78.25)

Especially be careful of "believing God" for someone you have a crush on. Or if someone approaches you and says "God told me that you are my husband or wife". Or if someone tells you, "I have a word for you - God told me that he wants you to marry so-and-so." This happens a lot today. At the least, it's non-biblical foolishness. And sometimes its actually witchcraft - attempting to control and go around someone's else's free will.

If you want the best - give up your own will, ask, and believe God to choose your mate. He will let you know which one. He will confirm it so that it is clear. You will also experience the tenfold anointing and supernatural power that goes with finding your true mate.

If you wonder what kind of marriage God wants you to have, it's spelled out in Philippians 2.2-4 NIV:

"Then make my joy complete by being like-minded, having the same love, being one in spirit and of one mind. Do nothing out of selfish ambition or vain conceit. Rather, in humility value others (your spouse) above yourselves, not looking to your own interests but each of you to the interests of the other (your spouse)."

It's not about earthly love, it's about destiny and the Will of God

Here is a good illustration of how God can pick the right person, when people cannot. The prophet Samuel was looking for who the Lord had picked to be the new King of Israel -

When they arrived, Samuel saw Eliab and thought, "Surely the Lord's anointed stands here before the Lord."

But the Lord said to Samuel, "Do not consider his appearance or his height, for I have rejected him. The Lord does not look at the things people look at. People look at the outward appearance, but the Lord looks at the heart." (1 Samuel 16.6-7 NIV)

Now let's take a look at this story and adjust it for when Bobby B Good a nice Christian boy meets Suzie Q the cute party girl one Sunday morning -

When he arrived at church that morning, Bobby B. Good saw Suzie Q and thought, "Surely the Lord's anointed stands here before me."

But the Pastor said to Bobby, "Do not consider her appearance or how fun she may seem, for she's got some issues. The Lord does not look at the things people look at. People look at the outward appearance, but the Lord looks at the heart. You're better off with someone who will appreciate you for more than your looks and if you can show her 'a good time'."

But Bobby B. Good said, "no! I don't care if she doesn't treat me right, she's so-o-o hot and wants to party with me !"

Fast forward a couple years, Bobby B. Good is alone again. Suzie Q ran off with another guy and now she's a single mom. Bobby's wondering "where did all the good girls go?" You know, the bible reading, quiet girls who wanted to date him before - here's where they are now - they all married good hardworking guys every one, and they have good marriages. While Bobby is looking across the room and seeing what he could have had... and now it's gone...

I took your father Abraham from the land beyond the Euphrates and led him throughout Canaan and gave him many descendants. I gave him Isaac, and to Isaac I gave Jacob and Esau. I assigned the hill country of Seir to Esau, but Jacob and his family went down to Egypt. (Joshua 24.3-4 NIV)

This scripture is interesting because it says Esau was also given by God like Jacob was. Even though later God says he hated Esau because Esau didn't accept God.

Isaac was from God, because God put Sarah and Abraham together. So when God puts two people together like Isaac and Rebecca most people would think that any children they have are from God also.

Yet we all know of truly good couples who have kids who get messed up.

The answer is simple, people have free will. Even if they have a great heritage from parents in a Marriage of Fire - they can still choose to go their own way. Esau despised his birthright as the son of Isaac. But Jacob chose the good path, obeyed his mother even when Isaac was about to miss it because of a steak dinner, and it says that God loved Jacob.

Spiritual Warfare Battle Plan:

This is especially hard in the day of so much wrong teaching about marriage - but it can be done!

If you want the husband or wife that God chooses for you and will be the best marriage partner you could have, then take these steps -

1. First, put your will on the altar. Give up your right to choose your own husband or wife. This may take some time, and you may have days when you want someone you just met, because "you like them and it would be quicker and easier, and you really want to get married". That's a good time to put your will back up on the altar.

2. Every day thank God that He is bringing you the husband or wife that He Himself has chosen for you. Tell Him that you give up your own will so you can get His Will.

3. Remind yourself that God knows everything. He also knows the future and how things will work out with your marriage years from now. These are things you cannot possibly know. Thank Him that He will bring you together with your future husband or

wife. He also knows where they are right now, they might be next door, or halfway around the world. He knows how to send angels to make a divine appointment for you to meet them.

4. Once you have given up your right to choose, and are believing Him to choose for you, then when you meet your husband or wife, God will make it clear to you - and also to your marriage partner.

5. After you are married, Paul says in 1 Corinthians 7.28 NIV that "those who marry will face some problems in this life". But you can rest assured that your marriage is the best marriage possible, and that your marriage has a real purpose, because it is God who has put you together.

Chapter 8

A Marriage that Cannot Be Shaken

Before we believers know what a purpose for our marriage is, we have to know our spiritual identity. Here is a good declaration of our identity: "Peter, an apostle of Jesus Christ, to God's elect, strangers in the world, scattered throughout Pontus, Galatia, Cappadocia, Asia, and Bithynia, who have been chosen according to the foreknowledge of God the Father, through the sanctifying work of the Spirit, for obedience to Jesus Christ and sprinkled with His Blood: Grace and peace be yours in abundance." (1 Peter 1.1-2 NIV)

We are -

God's beloved chosen people.

Strangers in the world - yet our spirits are firmly established in the Kingdom of God.

We have been chosen to do God's work.

We are being sanctified and purified by the consistent work of the Holy Spirit within us - which makes us obedient to Messiah and His will for our lives.

Peace is ours in abundance: "He was pierced for our transgressions, he was crushed for our iniquities. The punishment that brought us peace was on him, and by his wounds we are healed." (Isaiah 53.5 NIV)

Sometimes peace in our marriages can be shaken for whatever reasons, especially when we are living in the world full of unrests and strife, family issues, immorality, news media that slander those who they don't like, and bring lies into people's marriages. That's why it's important to build a marriage upon a solid rock as a foundation - which is God's purpose and calling for each marriage individually.

"The words 'once more' indicate the removing of what can be shaken--that is, created things--so that what cannot be shaken may remain." (Hebrews 12.27 NIV)

Things that cannot be shaken such as godly marriages remain. They keep growing stronger and stronger with each passing year.

What if you messed up and ended up in a divorce but still wish to have a good marriage with someone who God wants to pick for you? Should you be beating yourself up about it?

"He erased the certificate of debt, with its obligations, that was against us and opposed to us, and has taken it away by nailing it to the cross." (Colossians 2.14 HCSB) Any unfavorable record is done with after we repent and recommit ourselves to God to continue to live in the center of His will.

So how do we attain the peace within our marriages? What would you do if you wanted a very beautiful but expensive dress? You'd either set aside money each month as you work or you'll pester your husband so much about it that he's going to have enough of hearing about it and give in to your demand.

The principle is simple and it is this - be persistent: "But I tell you this -- though he won't do it for friendship's sake, if you keep knocking long enough, he will get up and give you whatever you need because of your shameless persistence." (Luke 11.8 NLT)

If we can shamelessly pursue increasingly expensive and worthless college degrees, buying a nice house, losing or gaining weight, and such material/physical/financial things, why should we shy away and not be bold and persistent in pursuing the peace within our marriage?

If we focus on fixing our own flaws first and continue making sure we are walking according to God's word and purpose for our lives, we'll have less time to create strife and more time to relax, live a blessed life, and pursue peace.

The strife in marriage comes from within the spouses themselves. Evil spirits play off of our insecurities, inconsistencies, and problems. Even if we didn't always have peace within our marriage, we can still turn it around because God's language isn't a language of death, but the language of resurrection.

Spiritual Warfare Battle Plan:

1. Start asking God for a resurrected marriage.

2. Start saying with your mouth out loud: "My marriage is resurrected! My marriage is born again in Jesus Name! My marriage cannot be shaken!"

3. Refuse to believe or accept anything less, regardless of what it looks like on any given day. Tomorrow is a new day.

How to Have Unity in Fighting Spiritual Evils

The enemies of our souls (evil forces) thrive on arguments and strife between spouses. The more of the strife we allow to go on for long periods of time, the more of a stronghold the devil is going to have in our marriages.

That's why it's so important to be "equally yoked" (2 Corinthians 6.14) with our spouse. What does being equally yoked mean when it comes to our spiritual lives? It means having a spouse who you can count on is going to help you battle evil forces in the world.

Husband and wife are supposed to be One Person: "The Lord God said, "It is not good for the man to be alone. I will make a helper suitable for him." (Genesis 2.18 NIV)

If a woman's husband is disobedient to God's Word and leadership, involved in strange spiritual practices, treats his wife in bad ways and vice versa, then there is no spiritual unity between those two souls and no unity when it comes to fighting devils because one spouse is already in their camp.

There are two types of lions described in the Bible, one is the devil himself: "Be alert and of sober mind. Your enemy the devil prowls around like a roaring lion looking for someone to devour." (1 Peter 5.8 NIV)

This verse tells us that the devil is actively positioning himself to capture a prey. He is after both a large and a small prey. It doesn't matter to him if he manages to capture a pastor or a baby christian, as long as he has some believer to devour.

Another kind of lion, a much stronger one is described in Hosea 13.7-8 NASB:

> "So I will be like a lion to them;
>
> Like a leopard I will lie in wait by the wayside.
>
> I will encounter them like a bear robbed of her cubs,
>
> And I will tear them open;
>
> There I will also devour them like a lioness,

As a wild beast would tear them.

It is your destruction, O Israel,

That you are against Me, against your help."

Here, the God of Israel is talking about His own strength. This lion seems to have the strength of several dangerous animals at once. Notice that no mention of any such strength was described to be in the first lion, the devil.

"Does a lion roar in the thicket when it has no prey? Does it growl in its den when it has caught nothing?" (Amos 3.4 NIV)

When the devil manages to capture someone in his teeth, he drags them in his den. And we can surely discern in which "lion's den" a person is by looking at the fruits that they produce.

We as believers have every right and authority and obligation to crush the necks of evil spirits and this should be one of our duties in the marriage. Consider the story of the unrighteous kings and how Joshua defeated them (we can relate this to evil spirits who are in high places and rule over areas, regions, countries, kingdoms).

Joshua conquered several cities and their kings and so a large city named Gibeon decided to simply surrender and make peace with Israel. The King of Jerusalem was jealous of what he had heard so he called upon several other kings to help him bring Gibeon to ruins. The citizens of Gibeon sent a message to Joshua while he was resting in his camp and begged him for help. Joshua was sought after because he was mighty in war. God assured him not to be afraid because the victory was guaranteed. God not only allowed Joshua and his warrior men to defeat the enemies, He even threw large stacks of hailstones against the enemies even though all the enemies tried to flee to another region.

Joshua had such favor with God that He even ordered the sun and moon to stand still until he defeated his enemies. God granted

Joshua his wish because God cared to free his righteous people from the Amorites and their blood thirst.

Joshua went back to the camp with his men but : "these five kings fled, and hid themselves in a cave at Makkedah." (Joshua 10.16 KJV) They tried to hide themselves from God's sight but someone told Joshua exactly where they fled. He ordered some men to roll a giant stone at the cave's entrance to make sure they stayed there until the appropriate time he was to deal with them face to face. Joshua was no coward, he was bold and unmoved by the power those kings had, he only cared about the power of his God.

"Then said Joshua, Open the mouth of the cave, and bring out those five kings unto me out of the cave. And they did so, and brought forth those five kings unto him out of the cave, the king of Jerusalem, the king of Hebron, the king of Jarmuth, the king of Lachish, and the king of Eglon. And it came to pass, when they brought out those kings unto Joshua, that Joshua called for all the men of Israel, and said unto the captains of the men of war which went with him, Come near, put your feet upon the necks of these kings. And they came near, and put their feet upon the necks of them. And Joshua said unto them, Fear not, nor be dismayed, be strong and of good courage: for thus shall the LORD do to all your enemies against whom you fight. And afterward Joshua smote them, and slew them, and hanged them on five trees: and they were hanging upon the trees until the evening." (Joshua 10.22-26 KJV)

Joshua and his war captains and all the other men of Israel were in agreement about destroying those evil kings. Joshua could've just killed them himself and take all the glory for himself personally, but he chose to give glory to God.

That's where his strength was: he relied on God, trusted in Him, and was bold when it came to obeying the voice of God.

Joshua said that God will crush the necks of all the enemies we fight. We are allowed to do what Joshua did, he and his men put their feet upon the necks of evil kings and ruined their influence forever. The kings are evil spirits which go against our assignments given to us from God, our marriages, our wellbeing, our relationship with God.

If a couple is in unity as these men were when they fought against evil kings, there is no high place of wickedness which can prevail against their prayers.

*We imagine that those warrior men for God
would pray a prayer like this:*

"God of Israel, You have promised to fight for us and promised that You will crush the necks of any and all enemies that fight against us. I believe in your promises and ask you to send your mighty warrior angels to chain every evil spirit who is in this area right now, to drag them into the deep and dry ground and close it above them, put chains around their necks so they cannot move, nor speak to anyone anymore until the Day of Judgement. I believe this is done in Jesus name."

Chapter 9

The Only Way to Pick a Church

The right church can help your marriage, while the wrong church can hurt it.

People in the USA pick churches in all kinds of ways, mostly silly. Some of these choices can also be ruinous to a marriage because sometimes the devils infiltrate churches and cause false teachings. That's why it's crucial to be filled with discernment and know what the Word of God has to say.

Let's start with the only real way to choose an assembly where your marriage will be fed spiritually -

David said in 1 Chronicles 16.27 GNT -

"Glory and Majesty surround him,
Power and Joy fill his Temple."

So - if there's no power or joy inside whatever church you are attending, then -

God's not there.

If there's a little bit of power or joy, then maybe He's there a little bit sometimes, but He's being crowded out by other things.

Happiness is not joy. Neither is emotion. Neither are shallow smiles. Joy is not easily shaken because it is a spiritual power rather than the fleeting feelings of a physical world.

Hopefully you can discern when joy is missing - people are stern or there is the "spirit of an annoyed English teacher", or it feels like you're in a country club with people in cliques rather than a spirit of unity and family.

Power is very obvious also - healings occur, devils are cast out, supernatural revelation and words of knowledge come forth at every service.

"Jesus replied, "You are in error because you do not know the Scriptures or the power of God." (Matthew 22.29 NIV) Any believer who doesn't spend time searching the Scriptures or spend time in the power of God is very likely to be deceived in one or more ways.

If rarely or never are laid hands on the sick for healing, there is no power. The same if demons are not rebuked off of believers on a regular basis. Demons don't take a vacation by the way - but a lot of churches don't bother with regular deliverance ministry - demons are quite at home in those churches because no one is challenging them.

When you come to the church you should "come to thousands upon thousands of angels in joyful assembly" (Hebrews 12.22 NIV). While the devil was judged 2000 years ago to suffer eternal hell (John 16.11). Just like married couples, the church goers should be united in spiritual warfare as one. Where power and joy are there will be lots of angels because they love the Presence of God - and He sends them as messengers to help us His children.

Here are good verses to declare over any demons that are troubling you or troubling your church:

"The Lord is going to make you weak, and no one will respect you. Your pride has deceived you. No one fears you as much as you think they do. You live on the rocky cliffs, high on top of the mountain. But even though you live as high up as an eagle, the Lord will bring you down." (Jeremiah 49.15-16 GNT)

Spiritual Warfare strategy:

Start looking for a good church as described in the scriptures in this chapter. Go there, get involved, and ask God to bless your marriage through this church.

Chapter 10

God Is Very Interested in Your Marriage

The God of the Bible is a truly abundant God. "Praise be to him who is able to do immeasurably more than all we ask or imagine, according to his mighty power that is at work within us". (Ephesians 3.20 NIV)

If you want the right man or woman to marry - God knows where he or she is. Even if that person is halfway around the world. Even if they grew up in a different culture, a different country (which was the story of Isaac and Rebecca).

Most likely, that right husband or wife is not on your list of "10 things I want in a mate", because no one is smart enough - or allknowing - to realize who is the best person for you. "I have come that they may have life, and have it to the full." (John 10.10 NIV) Jesus came so you can have a life better than you can imagine right now.

Do you want it or not? Are you willing to do what it takes to receive His gift?

"May the Lord, the God of your ancestors, increase you a thousand times and bless you as He has promised!" (Deuteronomy 1.11 NIV)

Can you even imagine what it would be like to have your life a thousand times better than it is now? Maybe start with believing for 10 times and work up from there.

Let's see some verses that put this into a better perspective:

"In My Father's house there are many mansions. And if not so, would I have told you that I go to prepare a place for you?" (John 14.2 BLB)

Living in a Heaven where you will want for nothing and not living in a simple house, but a mansion? A house would be just fine, but a mansion is more than enough!

"By His wounds you are healed." (1 Peter 2.24 NLT)

Not healed of some things, not healed every so often, but healed completely and all the time. Even before the health problems ever appeared you've already been healed from them. That's a divine health and it's more than enough! That's why we are to pray for the healing of others, our own healing, and receive it as God intends us to.

"The Lord is my shepherd; I shall not want". (Psalm 23 BSB)

If you let God lead you in life, not only will He fulfill all your needs according to the riches of his glory in Christ Jesus our Messiah (Philippians 4.19 BLB), but you will also have no wants. Isn't that amazing?

"The Lord is good to all; he has compassion on all he has made". (Psalm 145.9 NIV)

So many people believe for divine health, abundant finances, their family members to be saved, but how many believers believe for a marriage that's more than enough?

66

Why is it that people seem to just settle for problems in marriage, for the lack of communication, lack of care and selflessness, and accept these things as if that's how marriages should be?

As if God is too busy or disinterested to restore, heal, and renew your marriage?

God is very interested in every area of our lives, He yearns to have us connected to Him in all ways. We just seem to assume that somehow, marriage is our human issue to deal with and God has more important things to do anyways.

God is the one who established the marriage covenant. He created the original Marriage of Fire - why would He not care for how your marriage is working day to day? Why would He not desire to be involved in something that He has created?

Not only does He want to be involved - He is the God of Miracles - He is able to do whatever is needed to make things good and right.

Even sometimes believers get to some rough roads in their marriages, and either wife or husband brings in a third person as if that will somehow fix their lives.

The only "third person" that should ever be involved in your marriage is God. The God of Fire.

If you have lots of problems in your marriage day in and out but you have not asked God to be involved in your marriage and things seem to be falling apart though you and your husband are both saved, it may be you are dealing with a third "person" in your marriage as well, an evil spirit.

In Ezekiel 37.1-14, God is giving the prophet Ezekiel a vision of complete restoration. Dry and lifeless bones that have been scattered for a long time in a dry valley, come to life and are restored to be human beings yet again.

Everyone knows about the story of a young man named Lazarus

who had been dead for four days and was restored to life by Jesus.

If God can bring dead bones and dead people to complete restoration to life, why wouldn't He do the same for your marriage?

Jesus healed a woman who had been suffering with bleeding issues for twelve years (Matthew 9.20-22). Why wouldn't He do the same for issues in your marriage?

He also healed a woman who couldn't stand straight for eighteen years even when the pharisees refused to heal her with their constant procrastination and unbelief. (Luke 13.10-13)

If Jesus Christ is the same yesterday, today, and forever (Hebrews 13.8) and we know He is, then why would he not want to heal your marriage?

If God can renew your youth like the eagle's (Psalm 103.5) and He can renew our physical strength so that we can soar on wings like eagles, run and not grow weary, walk and not faint (Isaiah 40.31), why wouldn't he want to renew your marriage?

What are the steps to take in order to restore, heal, and renew your marriage?

1. Get into the covenant of agreement with your spouse. One can put a thousand to flight and two can put ten thousand to flight. (Deuteronomy 32.30) The Power of Agreement is strong because you together are One Person, One Flame of Fire in front of God.

2. After you have agreed in front of God that your marriage can be restored, healed, and renewed, set goals about how you will improve this marriage. God expects us to do our part as well. Creating a marriage that's more than enough is not a one prayer solution or a one day quick fix, it's a process, but all the odds are on our side.

3. Believe for the things that you want to see come to pass in your marriage. You have to stay in joint prayer about your marriage.

4. Receive the results you have been working on. "If you BELIEVE, you will RECEIVE whatever you ask for in prayer." (Matthew 21.22 NIV)

What are the things you believe for in your marriage?

What do you want to receive?

"Whatever you ask in my name, this I will do, that the Father may be glorified in the Son." (John 14.13 NHEB)

"You may ask me for anything in my Name, and I will do it." (John 14.14 NIV)

Whatever you ask for in Jesus Name, this He will do.

Spiritual Warfare strategy:

1. Write a list of the things you want to see happen in your marriage. It can be whatever. You may want to communicate better, to have more time with each other, to understand each other better, to learn how to resolve issues faster. You may want your husband to be a better provider, to have a better job, you may want a bigger and better house, you may want your spouse to cut off some bad influences in his/her life, healing from past wounds, more financial blessings.

2. No matter what you desire and want for in your marriage, be it spiritual, physical, financial, emotional, practical, write it down so you won't forget it.

3. Ask and believe for those things because "Whatever you ask in my Name, this I will do, that the Father may be glorified in the Son."

Chapter 11

Biblical Marriages and Problems -

Asking God for Children

Elizabeth And Zechariah

Have you ever asked yourself how would the world be today if either problems, circumstances, issues, other people, or evil spirits managed to break apart certain marriages in the Bible?

There are plenty of truthful stories found in the Bible which clearly describe doubts and problems that arose in the midst of marriages which were God ordained.

One of such stories is about John the Baptist's parents. The Bible says that Zechariah and Elizabeth were both from the priestly tribe of Levi. Levites had no material possessions, God was their possession, and God was closely involved with the Levites. It isn't hard to figure out that this marriage was God ordained. The Bible says they "were righteous in the sight of God, observing all the Lord's commands and decrees blamelessly". (Luke 1.6 NIV)

Their following of the Law was not only good but blameless, spotless. Yet, they both aged together and had no children. Clearly, it was no fault of their own because they did everything right. They kept the commands close to their heart and served God with all their being.

I'm sure they both had some level of frustration they were dealing with as both young people when they got married, unable to have children when everyone else around them had several children. However, God's plan was not to give them an average child, but an extraordinary one.

The story says that Elizabeth was infertile and Zechariah was the priest in the Temple of God so his desire was to have a son who would be a minister to God just like he was. So he prayed and the angel Gabriel appeared to him with a message from God. The Angel told him that his son will be "great in the sight of the Lord". (Luke 1.15 NIV)

This was the same angel that God later sent to Mary (Luke 1.28).

So after all those decades, Elizabeth finally became pregnant and said that the Lord has shown his favor upon her (Luke 1.25). God's favor was so great upon Elizabeth that He even filled her with the Holy Spirit (Luke 1.41) though the day of Pentecost and Jesus' resurrection was yet to come!

So what if Zechariah just gave up and chose not to follow God's will for his life and divorced Elizabeth because she was unable to have children? What if the issue of old age and infertility had torn them apart? There would be no John the Baptist, who would be "called a prophet of the Most High" (Luke 1.76 NIV).

God's plan wasn't to bring disgrace onto them, but to bless them with an unusual, insightful, and remarkable child though they were both old. After all the problems they had endured, John's father prophesied over him:

"And you, my child, will be called a prophet of the Most High; for you will go on before the Lord to prepare the way for him, to give his people the knowledge of salvation through the forgiveness of their sins". (Luke 1.76-77 NIV)

At the end, those who spoke disgrace over Elizabeth (Luke 1.25) were disgraced and embarrassed themselves. "Let their lying lips be silenced, for with pride and contempt they speak arrogantly against the righteous." (Psalm 31.18 NIV)

Spiritual Warfare strategy:

If you're believing for a child, declare with your mouth every day:

We ask you God to bless us with an unusual, insightful, wise, and remarkable child who will belong to the Most High, and who will bring people the knowledge of salvation through Jesus.

Chapter 12

The Couple Who Raised the Messiah

Mary and Joseph

Why would God choose to place His Son, God in human form, with none else than Mary and Joseph? The answer is found in John 14.23 NIV, Jesus replied, "Anyone who loves me will obey my teaching. My Father will love them, and we will come to them and make our home with them."

This was taken literally when God chose Mary and Joseph's household to place His Son in. We can even say that God was looking for the best home which would spiritually adopt His Son while He was on the earth. Jesus was literally in the home with Mary and Joseph, so we can conclude that they loved God and obeyed His teachings. This is very important to God and, as the story unfolds, it becomes clear why.

Elizabeth's cousin Mary was a young woman who was engaged to be married with a descendant of David, named Joseph. Mary was keeping herself pure because she was still unmarried, she was a virgin. When the angel Gabriel appeared to her, he greeted her in an unusual way: "Greetings, you who are highly favored! The Lord is with you." (Luke 1.28 NIV)

So just like her cousin Elizabeth, Mary was not only favored, but highly favored in the sight of God. The Lord was with her. He chose Mary to carry the Savior because she was very worthy in His eyes. She was not rich and nowhere in the Bible does it say that she was a gorgeous woman, but she had a "gentle and quiet spirit" which God prizes highly in a woman (1 Peter 3.4).

So God was not focused on the external things on and around Mary, He looked at her spirit and was sure that she would not harm Jesus in any way nor cause Him to stumble.

While Mary was wondering and fearing about the kind of greeting she had just received (Luke 1.29), the angel spoke again and said: "Do not be afraid, Mary. You have found favor with God." (Luke 1.30 NIV)

He was confirming it yet again that God's favor was upon her life. Then the angel told her that she will bear the Son of God who will reign forever. She was curious about the process in which this was about to take place and the angel told her that she will become pregnant by the power of the Holy Spirit and the fiery power of God which will overshadow her. (Luke 1.35)

The angel also informed her about her cousin Elizabeth who was six months pregnant at the time and for whom the others said she was unable to have children (Luke 1.36). Notice that the angel never told Mary about the cousin YOU have said is unable to have children. That's because Mary would never say such a thing about her older cousin because her faith was great as is visible when she accepted the angel's words and said: "I am the Lord's servant. Let your word to me be fulfilled." (Luke 1.38 NIV)

74

God knew that Mary would accept the angel's words and agree on her part to conceive Jesus. God wouldn't have given His Son to some woman who would think she was hallucinating the angel or who was worshipping baal while cheating her husband with several men!

Mary was humble in her spirit (Luke 1.48) and loyal to God.

Mary spent several months with her cousin Elizabeth in another town and then she returned to her own hometown. Her husband-to-be Joseph was greatly troubled because it was clear that she was pregnant.

God knew this would cause any man a concern, because the woman he loved was away for a few months and all of a sudden she comes home pregnant. Any man would think she cheated on him behind his back.

But Mary and Joseph were a God-ordained Marriage of Fire and Joseph wasn't an average man. He "was faithful to the law" and didn't want to publicly disgrace Mary because he still cared about her. However, doubts soaked into his heart and mind and he "had in mind to divorce her quietly." (Matthew 1.19 NIV)

Why would he ponder about divorcing her when they weren't even married yet? Because in those times, if you were promised to someone, that covenant was as good as marriage because back then, people's words meant something. So he pondered to divorce her from the covenant that he made with her, which was to take her as his forever wife.

At this point, he was pretty sure that she had been cheating on him, and he felt hurt and betrayed. After his mind was set on the divorce, God got involved and sent His angel in a dream: "Joseph son of David, do not be afraid to take Mary home as your wife, because what is conceived in her is from the Holy Spirit." (Matthew 1.20 NIV)

Joseph wasn't going to let Mary live with him in their promised future home, but Joseph listened to the angel and did what the angel had commanded him to do, which was to love Mary and Jesus, who was no child of adultery but was of the Holy Spirit. So after that, Joseph got over a mad spell and "took Mary home as his wife." (Luke 1.24 NIV) He realized he made a mistake and accepted Mary back into his life.

It was very important for God to have Joseph given to Mary because if she had been with some man who didn't care about God or his commands and was abusive and violent on top of that, the poor woman would probably end up being beaten to death for simply obeying God.

When a husband is having trust issues and thinks his wife is cheating on him, it takes time for those thoughts to go away and heal. And no doubt Mary had to heal the thoughts inside of her head about her husband abandoning her during her pregnancy.

Even God-ordained marriages and unions may have some issues arise somewhere during the journey, simply because every human being is imperfect.

But a true Marriage of Fire, like Mary and Joseph had, endures all things and triumphs through love for each other and obedience to God.

Spiritual Warfare strategy:

Start praying that God will give you and your spouse the same spirit He gave Mary and Joseph, and that He will make your spirits two Flames of One Fire.

Chapter 13

Casting Out Darkness from Your Past to Have Light in Your Marriage

Sometimes we encounter some hard and dark things/events/experiences in our marriages. Everyone has certain things in their past - or even in their ancestors' past - which have not been fully dealt with. Sometimes we don't even know all the things that we're dealing with which can influence the present.

Our flaws and hurtful experiences of the past can get the best of us. Have you ever 'suddenly' said or done something that "wasn't you"? You're shocked and horrified that you said or did that. It's because there is some wound that needs to be healed or demonic thorn that needs to be removed.

In marriage we have to love our mate no matter what. We have to understand that they may not even be aware of all the things they are dealing with. And they have to give us the same space and love and help to heal those wounds and pull out those thorns. That's one of the grandest things of marriage - a male lion and a female lion removing each others' thorns from the other and licking each others' wounds.

Sometimes we may strive to look for the bright side, but attack after attack of the enemy and evil people or circumstances keep on showing up.

That is the time to go out to battle in the spirit realm. Man and woman in a union have 10 times the anointing as they had alone - they are well able to win over all adversaries and gain all dominion in every area which was God's plan for Adam and Eve. (Genesis 1.28)

God knew that we would have trouble in the world (John 16.33) and that we would need to be encouraged sometimes. We know that Jesus lived before the world was created, but how do we get the full picture of what it really means? The verses of John 17.5 ABPE translated from Aramaic paint the picture perfectly for us. "Now, glorify me, my Father, in union with Yourself, in that Glory which I had in union with You before (the light of) the universe was."

Before even a small ray of light was ever created, Father and Son, God and Jesus were naturally so bright that they could see each other even in the complete darkness that covered the entire world. "Now the earth was formless and empty, darkness was over the surface of the deep, and the Spirit of God was hovering over the waters." (Genesis 1.2 NIV) That's why we are also to be the Light of the world. (Matthew 5.14)

God is able to see through anything in the darkness even when we fail to see any hope, that's why it's so important to have eyes that see. (Matthew 13:16) God can give us supernatural sight so that we will not stumble in the darkness, because we can see like it is the light of day.

At the time of Jesus' crucifixion, Mary the mother of Jesus was a widow. She had already lost her husband and now she was watching one of her sons die. But Jesus was interested in his earthly mother's wellbeing because he selflessly pondered at the time of his death who would be the one to provide a living for her.

Mary was there with her sister, Salome, one of the three women who witnessed Jesus' resurrection. So Jesus gave Mary to Salome's son to care for her, John who was his cousin. "When Jesus saw his mother there, and the disciple whom he loved standing nearby, he said to her, 'Woman, here is your son, and to the disciple, Here is your mother.' From that time on, this disciple took her into his home". (John 19.26-27 NIV)

There is a lot of emotion in these verses. Mary was the best woman, and this is why God made her pregnant by the power of the Holy Spirit. She was a chaste and godly woman, and yet she endured such harsh experiences by losing her husband and son by an unjust and cruel murder. What Jesus gave her though is provision for the rest of her life, eternal life, and high standing among all women for all eternity.

A lot of 'church' people may not like this next statement:

The greater the righteousness, the greater the suffering - and the greater the rewards.

But is that really true? Why can't we just go to a 'country club church' and have all the blessings? Why can't we just join a churchian social club and avoid all that unpleasant and inconvenient suffering? That's so old testament anyway.

The men and women who were heroes in the bible - all had times of suffering. It just was never suffering for evil - because they were righteous. It was suffering inflicted by evil spirits who hate the righteous. These same biblical heroes also had blessings on this earth far greater than anyone else in their time.

You want to be blessed? Then you'll have to do what God wants. Even though demons will hate you, they will flee at the Name of Jesus.

The real problem is *people* who are influenced or controlled by demons - because people have free will which is much harder to deal with than demons.

That's because **God set up the free will of man and woman to rule the earth**. When human free will gets corrupted by evil spirits, it becomes the source of much, if not all the suffering on the earth.

In 2 Thessalonians 3.2 Paul said we should pray to the Lord about it, "that we may be delivered from unreasonable and evil people, for not all have faith." NHEB Another version: "that we would be saved from evil and vicious men, for the faith does not belong to everyone". ABPE

God is against every mountain in our lives and marriages. Every mountain that is weakening us, discouraging us, making us feel worthless and defeated:

"I am against you, you destroying mountain... declares the Lord. I will stretch out my hand against you, roll you off the cliffs, and make you a burnt mountain." (Jeremiah 51.25 NIV)

We can declare these verses every day over our personal mountains because God has made it His mission to destroy every stumbling mountain that hinders us!

If we only remain united to God's Word and His promises, we can declare and expect to have a marriage as blessed as Isaac and Rebecca's or as Mary and Joseph's marriage was. They are an example to us to show us what a Marriage of Fire looks like.

Spiritual Warfare strategy:

1. Declare with your mouth every day: God will remove every mountain in our lives and marriage.

2. Our marriage will be blessed like Isaac and Rebecca's and as Mary and Joseph's marriage was.

Chapter 14

The Power of God in Your Marriage Through the Anointing Oil of Fire

When God saves us, He saves us forever.

When He protects us, He continues to protect us forever.

He doesn't stop just because you may have screwed up somehow today.

He doesn't stop blessing us as long as we continue living in obedience to Him and His Word.

"I will take you to be my wife forever. I will take you to be my wife in righteousness, justice, love, and compassion. I will take you to be my wife in faithfulness, and you will know the LORD." (Hosea 2.19-20 CSB)

These verses can also be applied to the marriage, but only the marriage God has put together - a marriage of righteousness and justice, steadfast love and mercy, lasting faithfulness. That is what a Marriage of Fire is.

No, there isn't any marriage in heaven (Matthew 22.30) but if a couple walks in obedience to God's calling, their marriage can last in the earth and be blessed.

The thing is, such marriages will be greatly blessed, one hundred fold, with persecutions though. (Mark 10.30) Those are the turbulences in the marriage caused by the evil spirits or people's free will. "In that day," declares the LORD, "you will call Me 'my husband,' and no longer call Me 'my Master'". (Hosea 2.16 BSB)

Since we have all become Jews after getting saved (Ephesians 2.11-22) fellow citizens in one new people, (see the Amazon book *One New People* by Epstein) we need to do what the Bible says unconditionally. "From the high rocks I can see them. I can watch them from the hills. They are a nation that lives alone. They know they are blessed more than other nations." (Numbers 23.9 GNT)

You have to know your marriage shall be more blessed than other people's marriages.

As Christians we have no excuse because our ancestors the Jews were more blessed than any other nation that existed and they operated in the supernatural realms, so our marriages should operate in the supernatural realms as well.

Can blessings run out? Can they turn dry? Did God somehow forget about the promises He made to our ancestors?

The answer to that is the Anointing Oil of "the Festival of Dedication" (John 10.22-23) or Hanukkah which Jesus celebrated. After the war at that time, Jews had no time to replenish their supplies so only one jar of oil remained to reignite the Eternal Fire in the Temple. How many times do we win a spiritual battle after a long fight and we have no rest but have to push forward even if all our supplies - like strength and faith - have been used up? But a miracle happened and the oil continued to light the Temple for eight days.

God did another miracle with the poor widow's small jar of oil that continued to flow. (2 Kings 4.1-7)

If God is for your marriage, who can be against it? (Romans 8.31) Not people and not even evil spirits: "I have given you authority to trample on snakes and scorpions and to overcome all the power of the enemy. Nothing will harm you." (Luke 10.19 NIV)

<u>Spiritual Warfare strategy</u>:

Start making this declaration every day with your mouth -

The Anointing Oil of the God of Israel, the God of Fire, is poured on our marriage for protection, provision, and blessings that never run dry, because they are constantly replenished and restored like the Living Waters. God is Anointing our marriage with His Holy Oil, and it will never run dry and never lose its power.

Submission - True Meaning

There are some believers who use Scriptures to put a yoke on women and think they are understanding the Bible correctly. Some believers think a woman should submit to her husband no matter what, no matter if he's beating her, cheating on her, deceiving her, being a drunkard, wasting money on frivolous things, putting her down, not taking care of her, etc. If God expected women to do that, would He inspire an apostle to write this down: "Wives, submit yourselves to your own husbands *as you do to the Lord.*" (Ephesians 5.22 NIV) So are female believers submitting themselves to Jesus who was an abuser, cheater, deceiver, drunkard, etc.? Jesus is the image of how a man should be in marriage, it's just that those men who say these false things about submission are not living their lives according to the Bible and are hoping that some women would be foolish enough to let them do whatever they want and stay submitted to them no matter how bad they become.

"Now as the church submits to the Messiah, so also wives should submit to their husbands in everything." (Ephesians 5.24 NIV) There are many women who love the Lord therefore proving that women are fine with submitting to a good and godly role model, but no woman should ever submit herself to the leadership of the devil, which is the man who claims to be a believer and is not leading his life in godly ways and is beating women over the head with the word submit.

Submission can only come either out of love or out of fear. But the Bible says: "There is no fear in love. Perfect love drives out fear, because fear has to do with punishment." (1 John 4.18 NIV)

At the same time, the Bible also tells husbands this: "Husbands, love your wives, just as our Messiah loved the church and gave himself up for her". (Ephesians 5.25 NIV) Giving himself up for her is another way of saying humble your lives for your wives. "There is no greater love than to lay down one's life for one's friends." (John 15.13 NLT) God says that husbands need to love their wives with the greatest of love.

Giving yourself up for your wife means making sacrifices. Means working three jobs if you have to, means going to the shopping mall when you hate it, means staying up at night and praying for your wife, means allowing her to have multiple pets even if you don't like them all, etc.

"In this same way, husbands ought to love their wives as their own bodies. He who loves his wife loves himself. After all, no one ever hated their own body, but they feed and care for their body, just as Messiah does the church". (Ephesians 5.28-29 NIV)

Just as Messiah Jesus feeds and takes care of the church, so a husband needs to feed (spiritually, materially) his wife and take care of her. Men who don't love their wives don't love themselves because if God put them together, they became one flesh and someone who doesn't love his own flesh doesn't love himself. Submission isn't a one way street as some would have others believe. The Bible calls this "a profound mystery". (Ephesians 5.32

NIV)

However, sometimes it so happens that a woman is the one who ends up being saved in the marriage first and then her husband, in this case the Bible says: "You married women, in the same way, must be submissive to your husbands, so that any who refuse to believe the message may be won over without argument through the behavior of their wives". (1 Peter 3.1 AAT) This only works if the husband is open to the Lord's message in his heart. A man who is jaded and has a heart of stone will refuse to listen to the Holy Spirit even if he has the best wife in the world. God is specific in the ways each must behave in the marriage: "Each one of you also must love his wife as he loves himself, and the wife must respect her husband." (Ephesians 5.33 NIV)

If this was common behavior for both genders, it wouldn't have to be written in the Bible for the whole world to see and emulate. Men have a hard time loving their wives and women have a hard time respecting their husbands, yet this is what God expects from each gender. Men must love their wives with the greatest love and wives must respect their husbands with the greatest respect.

We'll have more to say about this in Chapter 16.

Chapter 15

A Well Respected Woman With the Power of God

The Story of Deborah

Both the husband and wife have to have the right spirit in marriage.

A godly man needs a wife who has the spirit of Deborah. When it comes to men, you ought to not marry (or maybe stay married to) an unrepentant Jezebel just because you already made a mistake to get involved with her.

A 'Jezebel' is a woman whose heart is snares and nets, who seeks to control by any means possible (this is witchcraft). She is not capable of letting go and trusting her husband.

Whereas when a woman has the spirit of Deborah, the heart of her husband can trust safely in her.

"Can a mother forget the baby at her breast and have no compassion on the child she has borne? Though she may forget, I will not forget you!" (Isaiah 49.15 NIV) This is a feminine part of God speaking and it shows the right spirit a woman needs to have.

There's a lack of this spirit even in churches today and it is visible by mothers who either abandon or abort their children, which means that the spirit of motherhood isn't in them but an evil spiritual concept or ideology has taken the place where God's Word should be. If we women abandon our feminine qualities in order to compete with men or try to be like men, then we always lose. Men however need to be discerning and not get involved with women who lack this spirit because they may abandon or abort their children. Or abandon their husband or abort his potential in God.

But there is a woman in the Bible who had the right spirit in her. She was a prophetess, judge, songwriter, wife, singer, and a spiritual mother. **"Life in the villages ceased, it ended in Israel, until I, Deborah, arose, a mother in Israel."** (Judges 5.7 BSB)

What good man would not greatly desire a women like that?

Deborah was a well respected woman who had the power of God within her. God used her to restore Israel and save them from a warring tyrant.

We see that Deborah had an insight that it was her caring spirit of motherhood that God used to bring villages back to life and Israel back to security.

So how does a man make sure that he marries a woman with the spirit and strength of Deborah instead of the cunningness and deceit of Jezebel?

It has everything to do with giving up your will:

So he said to me, "This is the word of the LORD to Zerubbabel: 'Not by might nor by power, but by my Spirit,' says the LORD Almighty." (Zechariah 4.6 NIV)

This is the blueprint of how to "choose" a spouse. Not by might (not because you can and you have a right to), not by power (not by forcing, coercing, nor talking someone into it), but by God's spirit.

By allowing God's spirit to make this decision for you and by you giving up your will fully.

The problem is that churches have allowed secular culture that has nothing to do with the Bible to creep into the hearts and minds of sheep and pollute their view and understanding of the scriptures when it comes to marriage. A lot of times our thinking is like a flower in a tiny flower pot. The roots won't grow any further than what the pot can hold. God created us to spiritually grow without limitations we put on ourselves which bind our thinking into a rigid mold.

"Falling in Love"

The fact is that in the bible, what modern culture teaches about "falling in love" and then marrying that person, is a sure way to failure and grief because it contains no discernment and no Spirit of God but only the spirit of flesh. If you're a man, you want to have a woman with the anointing that Leah had, and if you're a woman, you want to be a woman like Leah was, then God will bring you to the right man for you. The right man will be a man like Abraham, Isaac, Jacob, John, Joseph. A man who may not be perfect, but who serves God and seeks His Will all the time. A man who can recognize when he's wrong and change. A man who understands the true value of a righteous woman like Deborah.

Be careful about obsessing over someone because that's not a spirit of God. "In the course of time, Amnon son of David fell in love with Tamar, the beautiful sister of Absalom son of David." (2 Samuel 13.1 NIV) Amnon had continuous obsessive and possessive thoughts about his half-sister, then an evil friend advised him to act upon them and rape his sister, which ruined her life and ultimately brought the death penalty upon himself.

Same thing happened to the daughter of Leah and Jacob. "When

Shechem son of Hamor the Hivite, who was chief of that region, saw her, he took her and raped her. But he found the young woman so attractive that he fell in love with her and tried to win her affection". (Genesis 34.2-3 GNT)

Same thing happened to Samson. "Some time later, he fell in love with a woman in the Valley of Sorek whose name was Delilah". (Judges 16.4 NIV)

Are you beginning to see the correlation between falling in love and death?

Why do you think the divorce rate is so high in this country?

Could it be because so many people are obsessed with "falling in love"?

With 'getting the spark'? Since it is simple biology that 'the spark' ends in a year, maybe two at most, there is no chance of ever having a marriage where the 'spark' keeps going beyond that.

Some people have figured that out, so many now just skip marriage, live together until 'the spark' fades, then move on to another spark-infested dead-end relationship.

Regardless of what you see in movies, what 'your friends are doing', even what you may hear in church sometimes - it's quite clear from the examples in the Bible that "falling in love" is the first sign of an impending divorce - or worse...

There is no perfect marriage on this earth. But your marriage can be God ordained, and you can be blessed and truly happy.

The Story of Ruth

A Virtuous Woman

Everybody thinks of Proverbs 31.10-31 when they think of a virtuous woman. Every decent man wants such a wife. The definition of a virtuous woman is clearly defined in those verses. If asked, most believers would say that the Bible called Mary a virtuous woman, because after all she was the mother of the Messiah and she was virtuous. But the truth is, there is only one woman in the Bible that the word virtuous was given to and it was Ruth.

The first thing that is clear about Ruth was that she became a widow early on and that she was a Moabite. Her husband was from the tribe of Ephraim. Though some people think that she was not a Jew, it is not confirmed to be so by the Bible -

"The days are coming," declares the Lord, "when I will punish all who are circumcised only in the flesh—Egypt, Judah, Edom, Ammon, *Moab* and all who live in the wilderness in distant places. For all these nations are really uncircumcised, and even the whole house of Israel is uncircumcised in heart." (Jeremiah 9.25-26 NIV)

So clearly, some ancestors of the Moabites were Jewish. After all, Ruth's mother in law and her husband and her two sons were Jews living in Moab. Ruth is listed in the line of Messiah (Boaz, Obed, Jesse, David, etc.) so it could also be another sign that her true identity was that of a hidden Jew.

However, Ruth and her sister in law were unbelievers. "Look," said Naomi, "your sister-in-law is going back to her people and her gods. Go back with her." (Ruth 1.15 NIV)

But Ruth was determined not to return to her hometown. Why would she do that? Maybe because she figured there was nothing there for her anymore, or because she didn't want to be reminded of her past. Why would she cling to her ex-mother in law so strongly? Maybe Naomi was the first person to show true kindness to her. Naomi was a mother figure to her. Maybe her own mother was abusive or maybe she lost her mother when she was just a child.

When they returned to Naomi's hometown, Ruth wanted to provide a living for herself and Naomi as soon as she could. God's favor brought her to a grain field that belonged to Boaz, her deceased husband's cousin.

She worked the hardest of any other worker in the field. "She came into the field and has remained here from morning till now, except for a short rest in the shelter." (Ruth 2.7 NIV) She could've been depressed about her husband's death or about the fact that she had to work for a living now or that she had to work under the heat of the sun, but she kept going because she decided to be strong and hopeful, no matter the circumstances.

She worked the entire day picking leftovers on the ground, she wasn't there to work for a paycheck, she just wanted some food at the end of the day. Her entire day was spent in a back breaking job just to gain a bit of food for herself and Naomi. The owner of the field saw that she wasn't there to interfere with anyone's work and she wasn't there to steal, so she found favor in his eyes. "My daughter, listen to me. Don't go and glean in another field and don't go away from here. Stay here with the women who work for me. Watch the field where the men are harvesting, and follow along after the women. I have told the men not to lay a hand on you. And whenever you are thirsty, go and get a drink from the water jars the men have filled." (Ruth 2.8-9 NIV)

As soon as she accepted the God of Israel by saying to Naomi "Your people will be my people and your God will be my God." (Ruth 1.16 NIV), her blessings immediately started to increase. "When she sat down with the harvesters, he offered her some roasted grain. She ate all she wanted and had some left over." (Ruth 2.14)

There was more than enough food when just a few days ago, her and Naomi were escaping famine. She shared her food with

Naomi: "So Ruth gleaned in the field until evening. Then she threshed the barley she had gathered, and it amounted to about an ephah. She carried it back to town, and her mother-in-law saw how much she had gathered. Ruth also brought out and gave her what she had left over after she had eaten enough." (Ruth 2.17-18 NIV)

She worked during the entire harvest season, not complaining and living with her mother in law. Naomi wanted to secure a constant provision for herself and Ruth, so she advised her to seduce Boaz. She went to do what Naomi advised her to do. Of course, Ruth's character wasn't that of today's cheap women. She didn't even touch him once, she just slept by his feet. Later in the night, he was startled by her presence and she said: "I am your servant. Spread the corner of your garment over me, since you are a guardian-redeemer of our family." (Ruth 3.9 NIV)

Garment has several meanings: some garments were used to cover nakedness like with the Levites in the Temple, so she may have felt she was uncovered by not having a husband to cover her spiritually. Garments are also symbols of a new life and beginning: believers are going to wear garments as white as snow in heaven - "Then one of the elders asked me, 'These in white robes--who are they, and where did they come from?'" Revelation 7.13 NIV). Garments are also spiritual virtues - "As God's chosen people, holy and dearly loved, clothe yourselves with compassion, kindness, humility, gentleness, and patience". (Colossians 3.12 NIV)

So what she was essentially saying was this - Please, just spread the corner of your garment over me, just show me a little bit of compassion, kindness, gentleness. She didn't ask for the whole thing, she just asked for a corner, a small provision.

Boaz was amazed at her act and her humility. He called her "a virtuous woman." (Ruth 3.11 NLT). He said that if another closer relative he knows of won't marry her, then he will. When the dawn arrived, he blessed her some more. "Bring me the shawl you are wearing and hold it out." When she did so, he poured into it six measures of barley and placed the bundle on her." (Ruth 3.15 NIV)

Boaz went to speak with the man who was first in line to claim Naomi's land that she was selling. The man wanted the land immediately, but he didn't want to marry a woman attached to it. So Boaz decided to marry Ruth, which is what he wanted to do anyways.

Naomi continued to be involved with both Ruth and Boaz after they got married. She even cared for their son because it gave her comfort after losing her own two sons.

How do we know that the author of Proverbs 31 didn't have the character of Ruth in mind when he wrote about what makes a virtuous woman?

Spiritual Warfare strategy:

If you want a Marriage of Fire, you're going to have to -

Give up your own will.

Wait for the Will of God.

And you're going to have to reject popular culture's idea of 'falling in love' if you want to avoid pain, misery, and destruction.

Do those things, then start saying every day - I believe that my marriage will be anointed by God and will be blessed and truly happy.

Believe the Lord for a Deborah or a Joseph or a Ruth or a Zechariah.

Chapter 16

Is the Greek Word for "submission" a Mistranslation?

What Does "submission" Mean in Hebrew?

Many scholars believed that the New Testament was written in Greek.

Then in 1947 the "Dead Sea Scrolls" were discovered by a Bedouin shepherd at Kumran near Jerusalem in Israel, where clay pots in caves were found to have preserved ancient manuscripts of the New Testament Bible written in Aramaic. Aramaic is Hebrew words written in Arabic letters.

Aramaic was the language spoken by Jews living in the Holy Land at the time of Jesus.

So some scholars began to realize that the New Testament may actually have been written in Aramaic originally - then translated into Greek to take the Message beyond Israel to the Greeks and the Romans (many of whom also spoke Greek).

Their reasoning was based on the question "why would people who spoke Aramaic write manuscripts in Greek"? Especially if they did not know Greek in the first place? Also, many differences in the Aramaic text compared to the Greek text, appeared to suggest that the Aramaic came first, then the Greek.

This all becomes even more interesting when you look at Ephesians 5.22 - a verse that has caused a lot of controversy and issues in churches over the years -

22 Wives submit (this word is actually *omitted* in many manuscripts) to your own husbands as to the Lord. (BSB)

The Greek word translated "submit" is hupotassó. The same word is also found in verse 24, relative to all of our relationships to Messiah. The meaning of this Greek word - to arrange under, submit, to place or rank under, to subject, to obey - are all things we as believers are expected to do - arrange our lives under His Word, submit to the yoke of Messiah, rank lower than our Teacher, place under and subject our flesh to discipline, obey the Word.

Since some manuscripts do not contain the word 'submit' at all, it is possible that the Greek manuscripts which have that word in Ephesians 5.22, were trying to "make it clear" by inserting the word where it actually did not appear. Who knows.

Accordingly, Ephesians 5.22 might also correctly read -

22 Wives *arrange yourself properly, under God's arrangement, to your own husbands* as to the Lord.

24 Now as the church *arranges itself* to Christ *under God's arrangement,* so wives to their husbands in everything

The Greek word hupotassó was originally a military term which meant "to arrange soldiers under a leader". In day-to-day life, it was used to mean "a voluntary attitude of giving in, cooperating, assuming responsibility, and carrying a burden".

We have the picture of believers in the "Army of the Lord" - and also believers cooperating with each other. In a marriage, both husbands and wives ideally will defer to one another, respect the others' wishes, cooperate with each other, assume responsibility for different areas of the marriage, and carry each others' burdens.

That insight into the Greek is amazing - but there is an even bigger picture here -

If the newer scholars are right that the Aramaic manuscript is the original, and the Greek manuscript is actually a translation from the Aramaic -

Then it becomes important to look at the Aramaic *source* to find out what word was used in the original manuscript - because that was the word which was translated into Greek, and then into English as "submit".

Here's where things get really interesting.

The Aramaic text of Ephesians 5.22 uses the verb כנע (kana').

The Hebrew verb כנע (kana) used in Ephesians 5.22 is sometimes translated "submit", but more fundamentally, this verb can describe the process of "merging" which is related to what Jesus said in Mark 10.8 about "oneness". When you discover the deeper meaning of this verb, you will have an "aha" moment.

The noun which derives from this verb is the feminine noun כנעה (kin'a), which can mean a bundle, wares, or merchandise (the same word is also used in Proverbs 31), or belongings - according to four different translations of Jeremiah 10.17 -

Pick up your bundle from the ground, You who dwell under siege! (NASB)

Gather up your wares out of the land, O inhabitant of the fortress. (KJV)

Gather up your belongings from the ground you who live under siege. (BSB)

Gather from the land your merchandise, O dweller in the bulwark. (YLT)

When you pick up a bundle, when you gather your belongings, the picture is of gathering them up as a bundle together in your arms and holding them tight.

This picture reminds us of Matthew 23.37 NASB "How often I wanted to gather your children together, as a hen gathers her chicks under her wings..."

In Arabic the word "kana" means to fold wings like an eagle. That reminds us of a majestic eagle settling down on her nest.

Don't women naturally want to do this?

In this book, we propose the idea that this is what the underlying Aramaic original of Ephesians 5.22 may actually be talking about.

Increase in Spiritual Power When Two Become One

In physics there is a process called "nuclear fusion" where two atoms merge. When that happens, a tremendous amount of energy is created, far more than either atom alone - that is how a hydrogen bomb works - a small amount of atoms creates an awe inspiring release of energy.

So it is with marriage. When two merge and become one, the supernatural power and anointing which is released is far greater than would be expected from either one of those two people alone.

Ecclesiastes 4.12 (GNT) says that "Two people can resist an attack [by the devil] that would defeat one person alone." And if you have the Holy Spirit in your marriage, you can win against major demonic assaults: "A rope made of three cords is hard to break."

Leviticus 26.8 NASB promises those Married in the Jewish Messiah that "Five of you will chase a hundred, and a hundred of you will chase 'ten thousands'".

The Hebrew word translated as 'ten thousands' is 'rebabah' which literally means 'myriad' (uncountable). This supernatural principle is found in other verses also. When believers unite - including two believers united in Marriage - their power increases exponentially.

1 Chronicles 12:14 NIV "These Israeli Gadites were army commanders; the least was a match for a hundred, and the greatest for a thousand."

Deuteronomy 28:7 NIV "The Lord will grant that the enemies who rise up against you will be defeated before you. They will come at you from one direction but flee from you in seven directions."

Zechariah 12:8 NIV "On that day the LORD will shield the people of Jerusalem. The weakest among them will be as mighty as King David! And the house of David will be like God, like the Angel of the LORD who goes before them!"

Judges 7.12, 19 NIV "The Midianites, the Amalekites, and all the other eastern peoples had settled in the valley, thick as locusts. Their camels could no more be counted than the sand on the seashore... when Gideon and the hundred men with him reached the camp."

Gideon and only 100 men defeated an uncountable myriad. Two believers united in a Marriage of Fire can defeat many strong enemies. In case they need extra help, there are myriads of angels that God can send to help us -

Revelation 5:11 NIV "Then I looked and heard the voice of many angels, numbering thousands upon thousands, and ten thousand times ten thousand."

This is the Heavenly host of Angels that God will send to help us fight.

2 Chronicles 32:7 BSB "Be strong and courageous! Do not be afraid

or discouraged before the king of Assyria and the vast army with him, for there is a greater One with us than with him. With him is only an arm of flesh, but with us is the LORD our God to help us and to fight our battles."

This is what a Marriage of Fire looks like - together, merged as one, aligned with Yeshua - they can fight against a myriad of demons and win with the Sword of the Spirit which is the Word of God.

Alignment is what happens when the Nations, which are described as "branches from a wild olive tree" Romans 11.17, are merged into the Jewish olive tree. This allows people from any country to enter into citizenship with the Holy Nation of Israel.

In the same way, a single woman for the sake of two people merging into a marriage, aligns herself with her husband and he with her, for their mutual benefit and blessing.

Husband and wife learn to speak the "same language", you've heard of couples who can "finish each other's sentences".

A single woman, to gain the blessings of Oneness, gives up her natural free state, which some feminists see as a loss of freedom. The single man gives up many of his options. But the freedom and spiritual power gained by gathering together, alignment, and Oneness is far greater.

In Genesis 11.6 they had the same language and vocabulary. The Lord said that because they have learned to do things as one people, all having the same language, then nothing they plan to do will be impossible for them.

Man and Woman can have this in marriage. _**They can reach a place in agreement where nothing they plan to do will be impossible for them**_. That is a Marriage of Fire.

Of course the people in Genesis 11 were not believers, so God stopped them by confusing their language so that they could not understand one another's speech. After that, they were scattered throughout the earth, and they stopped working together. That's why it is called Babylon, also found in Revelation.

The devil always has to copy God and twist what is good, because they devil cannot create, he can only destroy.

If you look at marriages in America today, you will see the devil copying what happened to Babylon. He confuses the language of husbands and wives, so that they talk past each other, interrupt each other, yell at each other, and cannot understand what the other one is saying.

When a couple stops speaking the Word of God because they can't understand each other anymore, that leads to their marriage being scattered, and eventually that ends in Splitsville.

The strength of even the unbelievers in Babylon was in direct proportion to their level of agreement and working together.

How much more when husband and wife are in agreement and can chase 10,000 demons anytime.

It's also interesting that the Hebrew word for "align" is שׁי "yisar". This root is found in the word "Yisarel" which we know as "Israel". It can literally mean "to align yourself with God".

Genesis 2.24 says that Man and Woman shall be "one flesh", or in Hebrew, "basar echad".

The Hebrew word for "together" is יחד "yachad" which is also the root word for "echad" or "one" used in "one flesh".

Are you "together" with your husband? Is he "together" with you?

Are you One with each other?

Are you Aligned with each other?

If so, you will be able to do awesome things in the supernatural.

That's a guarantee from the God of Israel who is the Word of God, the Word made Flesh.

The Hebrew idea of being aligned, together, synchronized with each other - One - is also a great roadmap for how men should relate to God. We men can bring ourselves into alignment together with Yeshua, holding fast to Him as our forefather Jacob did, refusing to let Him go until He blesses us.

Aligning Together as One

In the Hebrew, the deeper meaning of Ephesians 5.22 is for the woman to gather up her husband with love and protection - and her husband with her - as they bring their marriage relationship into alignment close together with each other and together with God.

And isn't this exactly what believing women want to do anyway?

What if this is what was taught in our churches?

Both Man and Woman could happily embrace the deeper Hebrew meaning of 'kana' - because it leads to a strong marriage, harmony, order, close alignment, and mutual benefit.

It's also interesting that the Greek word "ephalé" (ef-al-ay') (or kephalé kef-al-ay') referring to 'husband' in Ephesians 5.23 and which is translated "head" - also has a deeper meaning:
"a cornerstone, uniting two walls". It can also mean "source".

The same word is used for Christ in that verse - "The Son is the source (kephalē) of the Body of Messiah".

Note that the Greek word for 'submit' can also mean 'respect', as in Ephesians 5.21 "submit to one another" so it could also be translated "respect one another."

The bottom line is - Every Husband should love his Wife as himself, and the Wife should revere and respect her husband.

Here's something you may not have heard yet in church -

Ephesians 5.22 must be read in the context of Proverbs 31

Paul would have been very familiar with Proverbs 31 and so he would not have said anything that conflicted with it.

The Hebrew "kana" found in Ephesians 5.22 can mean a merchant or merchandise. This word is found in Proverbs 31 *three times* -

The Virtues of a Noble Woman

Who can find a virtuous wife for her worth is far above rubies.

She is like the merchant ships (kana), from afar she brings her food.

She considers a field and buys it from her profits (as a merchant does).

She plants a vineyard.

She perceives that her merchandise (kana) is good.

She makes tapestry for herself. Her clothing is fine linen and purple.

She makes linen garments for the merchant (kana) and sells them supplies and sashes.

The law of kindness is on her tongue.

Her husband is also kind and he praises her.

Her husband is known in the gates when he sits among the elders of the land.

Charm is deceitful and beauty is passing but a woman who fears Yahweh she shall be praised.

Husbands, take note that she dresses very fashionably. It's your responsibility to make sure she is dressed in fine linen and purple.

Also note that if you want a woman like this, you have to be a man who is known in the gates, because that's what she deserves.

So when Paul wrote Ephesians 5.22 he would not have said or meant anything in conflict with Proverbs 31.

Also remember that Paul was a Jewish rabbi. The Jewish bible is full of hidden references which are clues to underlying hidden meanings. Since the Hebrew word "kana" is found in the Aramaic manuscript of Ephesians 5.22, it is natural to look for clues as to where Paul got the idea for that word -

Because "kana" is a key word found in the Jewish idea of the perfect wife described in Proverbs 31, Paul may have telegraphed what he was thinking of by using "kana" in the original Aramaic manuscript of Ephesians 5.22.

The word would have meaning in Aramaic for Jewish believers, yet would also fit perfectly into the culture of Greek marriages - because Paul knew he would need to write a Greek version of Ephesians to send to the Greek speaking believers in Ephesus.

After all, as a rabbi Paul spoke Hebrew (and thus Aramaic), as well as Greek (which he displayed at Mars Hill in Athens), and probably Latin as well while he was in Rome *since he was a Roman citizen -*

It's a very clever play on words that crosses cultural barriers, and fits in with Paul's stated mission of being "a Jew to the Jews and a Greek to the Greeks".

In Ephesians he was writing to believers in a Greek city (Ephesus) in today's Turkey. So in the Greek version of Ephesians 5.22 he could have been using shorthand for "don't try to boss your husband around" - *because that was the Greek custom at the time.*

In the Greek city-states, women had very little freedom. They could not leave their house without their husband's permission. They could not even visit a temple without their husband's permission.

But in her own home, a woman was the boss. She cooked and cleaned and sewed and raised the kids. Some women had servants to do some or all of the work for them. They ruled their central courtyard. They could sit outside and enjoy the day.

However in Sparta, some of the women had a more independent mindset. To some contemporaries outside of Sparta, there were some Spartan women who had a reputation for controlling their husbands.

So in Ephesians 5.22 Paul -

1. May have been speaking to some of the Spartan women by using the Greek word for "submit", even though the underlying "kana" carried echoes of Proverbs 31.

2. He may have been talking to other Greek women, by confirming that the "submit" they were already accustomed to, was fine.

3. Yet he left hidden clues that Jewish believers everywhere who read the Aramaic manuscript of Ephesians could recognize as the echo of "kana" with Proverbs 31.

Paul could have been giving his "rabbi's opinion" to the Ephesians, yet not a command (as in 1 Corinthians 7.6). Rabbis of the day were accustomed to teaching the people, many of whom could not study the scriptures for themselves. A rabbi's opinion was valued for insight into daily life.

Paul was certainly clever enough as a rabbi to give a clue about the underlying meaning by the use of the Aramaic "kana" in the Aramaic version of the Ephesians letter when he was speaking as a Jew to the Jews, then translate it into the Greek word "hupotassó" which reads as 'submit' in the Greek version of the letter which would fit into Greek culture because he was speaking as a Greek to the Greeks.

Proverbs 31 contains three instances of "kana" all of which mean "merchant" or "merchandise". Proverbs 31 describes the ideal Jewish woman.

So you can read Ephesians 5.22 together with Proverbs 31 this way -

The Ideal Wife

The ideal wife in the Jewish Messiah is the wife described in Proverbs 31 who aligns herself close together with and gathers up her husband with love and protection as in Ephesians 5.22.

...But that was not the ideal Greek woman of those days, which to most Greeks of that time would have been a woman who needed their husband's permission to leave the house and had very little freedom. Except for the few Spartan women who had a reputation for controlling their husbands - so they too would have understood that they should be more like other Greek women in that respect.

Covering and Control "doctrines" in Churches

What if the Greek word 'submit' is a mistranslation?

And what if the meaning of the actual original Aramaic word is more like "aligning together as One"?

Then what does that teach us about the common 'covering' and 'control' doctrines which are found in some churches?

The first marriage that God put together was in the Garden. It was the only one that started out perfect. And it showed that each person in a marriage has free will, and thus the capacity to mess things up.

That is a big lesson for us today. No matter how well suited two people are, they each have free will. And there is still a serpent on the loose trying to get them to use their free will to destroy their own happiness.

What is the solution that the Messiah brought? Yeshua (Jesus) talked about marriage as it "was from the Beginning". That is, when Adam and Eve were walking with God.

Also, that was when God brought Eve to Adam. The lesson is, first God has to put a marriage together, that's how a marriage between believers should start out.

Then Paul has this advice "women align/adapt/synchronize yourself with your husband."

And in Ephesians 5:25 Paul's advice for men is the Hebrew word אהב "ahav" - Love your wives as Messiah loves His people. Ahav means "to love, to burn".

(As a footnote, it's interesting that the English pronunciation of the Aramaic word for "love" is "hubbana" or "hubba", which sounds a lot like "husband" or "hubby". That Aramaic word means literally "lovingly" and "amorous").

The Man Must Love as well as Lead

There seems to be a lot of focus in today's churches about what "women should do", and not much about what men should do.

At least what Paul says that women should do, adapt to their husbands, is actually doable.

While what men should do - love their wives like the Messiah loves His people - is clearly impossible.

But that doesn't mean men shouldn't be aiming for that goal anyway.

What would that look like? Well, how does Yeshua (Jesus) treat us?

He's always patient, even when we are being obstinate, clueless, having a tantrum, slacking off, and generally being a handful.

So husbands should learn to display patience with their wives.

He's always there to be with us when we want to talk to Him.

We can ask him anything and He will do it for us.

It doesn't end there, but the men reading this may be getting a bit uncomfortable about now, so let's move on to something else.

Just know that the characteristics of God are how Paul says men are to treat their wives. Easy for him to say, he wasn't married.

One more thing - Yeshua is always leading us to higher ground - to fulfilling all our potential. He never stops helping us to be better, to go higher, to find more treasures in ourselves we didn't know existed.

What does Yeshua not do?

He doesn't boss us around like the household help, nitpick us when we make small mistakes, forsake us when we screw up more than a little, make us feel embarrassed and ashamed that we exist, or make us feel like we can never measure up.

So, men - the above few paragraphs are a good place to get started.

Because - it is never God's will for the husband to harshly dominate his wife, the wife to dominate her husband, parents to dominate their kids, or a pastor to dominate the congregation.

Men and Women were created to rule the earth together - not control each other.

Control and accusing of another person is a sign that evil is present.

The word 'devil' literally means 'the accuser'. Many Bible teachers have pointed out that those who try to control other people are practicing witchcraft.

That is because God has created Man and Woman in His image with free will. When someone tries to take away that free will, it is sorcery and witchcraft.

Some examples are -

> slavery of whole peoples
>
> families enslaved by debt
>
> wives beaten by their husbands
>
> children neglected, mistreated, and abused by parents
>
> nations kept down by their own governments
>
> husbands emotionally destroyed by their wives
>
> unfair imprisonment by police and the courts
>
> weak people taken down the road to hell by 'the wrong crowd'

All those are witchcraft.

Control, domination, demands for 'submission', stubborn refusal to do what the Bible says - have no place in a church, or in a believer's marriage, whether from the husband or the wife.

When the Bible says "Man" - it is speaking a singular word to describe a plural Being (*Man and Woman* as **One).**

Man is two triune (spirit, soul, and body) Beings (Man and Woman, Ish and Ishah) joined by Love. Man is made in the Image of God, a Triune Being Who Is Love.

So it's important to know what a healthy relationship/marriage looks like in the Bible. Who lived happily ever after - and why? Who didn't, and why? We've looked at that a little bit with the examples of God-put-together marriages in this book.

Man and Woman are Partners in Dominion.

Here is the very first thing God told Adam and Eve - it's interesting that this is the first thing He told *Adam and Eve together* – and it is the first command mentioned in the Bible which is directed at Man (Ish and Ishah) –

Fill the earth

And subdue it

You can't fill the earth without the Woman

And you can't subdue it without the Man

(But it is *not* the first thing He told *Adam* - which was 'don't eat the fruit of the tree of the knowledge of good and evil').

"Man" is *male and female together.* We saw this from the Hebrew words in Genesis.

But now today Man and Woman are distinct and separate species. Yet in the Garden together as One they made up the Being called 'Man'.

Adam and Eve had perfect prosperity in the Garden of Eden.

They wanted for nothing - it is a clear picture of God's perfect plan for Men and Women.

They had perfect health.

They had a daily relationship with God.

We can have those things again now, but only through the Jewish Messiah Yeshua (Jesus).

God said right away in Chapter 2 of Genesis that it wasn't good for Man (the male) to be alone. So He made Woman (the female) *from* the Man.

At that time, Man and Woman existing together as One was called 'Man - God's creation'.

Not every Man or Woman is married today as it was in the Beginning, so now part of mankind exists as single Men and Women. Paul for example was one of them. He chose that to avoid the problems in marriage that Man and Woman now face after the fall.

God wants Men to be masculine and not feminine and he wants Women to be feminine not men.

This is true Dominion as it is presented in the Bible.

When Man and Woman live in marriage the way God designed it, then they will rule together.

So quit demanding that your wife 'submit'.

And quit trying to tell your husband what to do.

Those are things the two of you are supposed to be *doing to the rest of the earth - not to each other.*

Love her as your Woman and respect her free will.

Speak to your Man in love and he will hear you more clearly.

Man, you are to -

Pray for

Provide for

Protect

your Woman.

Woman, you are to -

Lovingly minister to your Man's vulnerable emotional side (that soft place left when God took you out of his side).

If you're a Man – and God has given you a loving Woman who __*helps you achieve your potential as Man*__ – it would be so unfair to treat her wrong.

It's fair and fitting to Protect her – because she's so valuable to you, to Provide for her – because she spends her time taking good care of you, and to Pray for her – because you want to always be lifting her before the Throne since you want nothing but good things for her.

If you're a Woman – and God has given you to a loving Man who

Protects you, Provides for you, and Prays earnestly for you – it would be so low class to want to boss him around and tell him what to do all the time, right?

It would be so unfair to treat a good Man with anything less than Honor.

Help him achieve all his potential, support him all the time, and use your Woman soul to minister to that soft vulnerable spot near his heart where God took Eve from, and created all her daughters, including you.

The Man has to nurture and lead the Woman spirit soul and body - but *only* how it's laid out in the Bible - the way God covers His People.

Keep your Woman safe and make her prosperous.

Woman, you can bless your Man these ways -

Help him

Support him

Be by his side

Strengthen and pray for your Man

Be there when he needs you

Rejoice in his strength

Make your home a refuge he can be safe in

Lean on him

Let him carry you

Teach him by your behavior

Agree with him in prayer

Shouldn't believing Men be looking for a Woman who will be led (initiated) by, get in agreement with, respond to, and obey God with, a Man of God who cherishes, protects, and provides for her?

Would Women feel more secure if they lived within the boundaries of being loved, protected, and provided for by a Man who follows hard after God?

Would Women who are wives feel more fulfilled if they accepted that a main purpose in their married life is to minister to a Man, what only a Woman can give him?

Would Men who are husbands be more stable if they worked on being Men who love, provide extravagantly for, and make their chosen Woman feel secure - and at the same time accept the Woman's ministry to their emotions as part of God's plan?

Women - without you we would not have civilization.

And without Men - you would not have houses to live in and cars to drive. Or shopping either.

Men are called for Dominion - to rule the earth.

Women are called to help their Man - and rule alongside him.

Women and children are entitled to be free from fear - and it is Man's calling to protect them.

The Names of God are good examples for the actions and characteristics that husbands and wives can give to each other -

The Lord our Healer
Men and Women should pray for each other's healing, and speak healing words to each other.

The Lord our Banner
Husbands should protect their wives from all kinds of the enemy's attacks. Wives should be the champions of their husbands.

The Lord our Provider
Husbands should provide for their wives. Wives should provide a home of refuge for their husbands.

Here's another verse for men -

1 Peter 3.7 NJCV - You husbands, live with your wives with understanding, and hold them in honor with tenderness like delicate vessels, because they also will inherit with you the gift of everlasting life. Do this and you won't be hindered in your prayers.

The Aramaic word in this verse translated as "honor" has all of the following meanings -

> honor
>
> majesty, gloriousness
>
> dedication
>
> gift
>
> have interest in

114

Reading this list, it's easy to see how far our culture and churches have fallen in how women are regarded. These words are a reminder of what God had in mind in the Garden.

In the next Chapter, we will look at how you can apply these hidden meanings to your marriage.

Chapter 17

How You Can Have a New Covenant Jewish Supernatural Marriage

A Marriage of Fire

Agreeing to Always Agree

Here is the Secret of Secrets in having a rock solid marriage, filled with every blessing.

Are you in agreement with your spouse?

Two cannot walk unless they are agreed. So when you hear any spouse say about their spouse, "we have agreed to disagree", they are actually saying "we have come into agreement, to use our immense God given power of agreement - to disagree, thus making it impossible for us to walk together, and making sure our marriage will be less than it could have been - maybe even destroy our marriage".

"Agreeing to disagree" is a line in a script written by the devil.

Sounds good, like the tree in the Garden. But its end is the death of the potential of your marriage.

All the roads you could have walked in agreement, all the new things you could have discovered, all the problems you could have overcome, all the blessings you could have had.

The conductor of an orchestra keeps the orchestra synchronized *in time*. Systems that operate with all parts in agreement are *in sync*.

Agreement is an ironclad rock solid promise from Jesus the Messiah Himself -

Matthew 18.19 NJCV - Again I assure you with certainty, that whenever two of you shall agree on earth concerning any matter and every thing whatever that they shall ask, it shall be done for them from the Presence of My Father who is in the Heavens.

The summing up is that you always be in agreement and of One mind. (1 Peter 3.8) NJCV

What does this mean?

Simply this - when a married Man and Woman ask *anything* when they are in agreement - God Himself will do every thing they ask!

James the brother of Yeshua Jesus said, "you have not because you ask not". (James 4:2 KJV)

Maybe he was thinking of when Yeshua said, "Ask and it will be given to you, seek and you will find, knock and the door will be opened to you." (Matthew 7:7 NIV)

Every Husband and Wife can ask in agreement, and receive *every thing* they ask for!

Spiritual Warfare Battle Plan:

1. Agree to Agree!

2. About everything!

3. All the time!

4. If you can't get into agreement about something right away - keep working on it until you do get in agreement.

5. Read the Bible and see what it says about the subject you're working on.

6. Ask God to show you how to be in agreement on *any* thing -

7. Then you can ask *every* thing - and receive it.

Then you will be living in a Marriage of Fire.

57262824R00076

Made in the USA
Middletown, DE
28 July 2019